The Spiritual Formation of Seminarians

The Spiritual Formation of
SEMINARIANS

Learning to Live in Intimate
and Unceasing Union with God

JAMES KEATING

Foreword
Bishop Keith J. Chylinski

The Catholic University of America Press
Washington, D.C.

Copyright © 2025

The Catholic University of America Press

All rights reserved

The paper used in this publication meets the minimum
requirements of American National Standards for
Information Science—Permanence of Paper for
Printed Library Materials, ANSI Z39.48-1992

∞

Cataloging-in-Publication Data is available from the Library of Congress

ISBN (paperback): 978-0-8132-3958-3

ISBN (ebook): 978-0-8132-3959-0

Imprimatur: In accordance with CIC 827, permission to publish has
been granted on March 18, 2025, by the Most Reverend Mark S. Rivituso,
Auxiliary Bishop, Archdiocese of St. Louis. Permission to publish is an
indication that nothing contrary to Church teaching is contained in
this work. It does not imply any endorsement of the opinions expressed
in the publication; nor is any liability assumed by this permission.

This book is dedicated to:

Fr James Mason and Fr Paul Hoesing

Rectores Magnifici

And to Michelle Funke, Managing Editor of
IPF Publications, Omaha, Nebraska
in honor of her commitment to fashioning
the finest publishing resources in the service
of seminary formation.

CONTENTS

Foreword by Bishop Keith J. Chylinski ix

Preface xi

One   Developing the Vulnerable Heart of
the Catholic Man 1

Two   Initial Observations on Seminarian Prayer 29

Three   From Loneliness to Solitude to Communion.... 61

Four   Formed in Word and Sacrament 97

Five   An Ascetical Devotion 125

Six   Prayer and Ministry 155

Bibliography 183

Scriptural Index 195

Index 197

FOREWORD

As a seminary rector, any book about forming diocesan seminarians draws my attention. When it contextualizes that work in terms of living in union with the Triune God, it piques my genuine interest.

That interest stems from previously working with seminarians as director of counseling services. There I came to see clearly that their growth requires healthy introspection, guided by the Holy Spirit. As Pope Francis describes it, "the journey of priestly formation is a worksite" where the Spirit first seeks to "demolish" whatever prevents seminarians from "growing according to the Gospel" and then strives to "build up [their] life in accordance with Jesus' style and make [them] become new creatures and missionary disciples."[1]

On this "worksite," the spiritual director functions as a foreman. Dr. Keating knows well what that job entails. His book offers a clear blueprint for the task, laying out key elements of spiritual development in a contemporary vision of seminary formation.

---

1 Pope Francis, "Address of His Holiness to the Community of the Archepiscopal Seminary of Naples" (Feb. 16, 2024).

x • Foreword

That vision emphasizes relationships rather than "rules." It recognizes that seminarians enter with vulnerable hearts and muddled minds, thanks to the prevailing cultural ethos. Like other young adults, they seek stability, which they find only in relationship to Him who is "the way, the truth, and the life" (Jn 14:6). Cultivating that relationship through prayer and spiritual guidance, seminarians can overcome the existential loneliness common to all and embrace the joyful experience of solitude in communion with the Triune God.

By championing an integrated vision of formation—focusing on spiritual relationship, capitalizing on divine grace, and preparing for priestly ministry—the spiritual director serves an indispensable role in diocesan seminaries. Dr. Keating's extensive experience in this role is bringing long-term benefit to the Church. Grateful for his insights, I commend this book as a valuable guide to all who share in this sacred work.

The Most Reverend Keith J. Chylinski, DD

Auxiliary Bishop of Philadelphia
Rector, Saint Charles Borromeo Seminary

PREFACE

The book is not a "how to" manual. It is an opportunity for one spiritual director to introduce his mind to the minds of other directors with the hope that his ideas may season their own already developed method of direction. I have not attended to all the possible realities a director may encounter within his or her training or within the daily execution of this ministry. There are many books on spiritual direction that we can further engage. Some are listed in the bibliography. In these pages, I wish to share my approach to directing seminarians by reflecting upon themes and experiences which regularly appear within direction sessions. My experience is with diocesan seminarians, although when I worked at the Institute for Priestly Formation (IPF), I also encountered men in formation for the religious priesthood, and I hope this book will be useful to religious spiritual directors as well.

Spiritual direction certainly has some universal components to it. All directors want their directees to internalize a habit of prayer, to choose a life of remaining with God, to suffer the vulnerability necessary to know divine love, and to then embody that love as heralds of the Gospel. But each director approaches his or her directees from within their own skin, from within a personality that is singular, and by way of a formation that reflects the individual attractions of each director and his or her own sufferings, failures, and fidelities. These unique embodiments no one writer can know or capture in a book. And so, this book simply begins a conversation that the author invites other directors to enter into and add to according to their own insights. I would hope the margins of this book's pages become filled with affirmation and appropriation, delight in discovering a sympathetic thinker or practitioner, critique and disagreement to round out this author's weaknesses or omissions, and perhaps some gratitude from the reader for having engaged in a way of direction that one had not thought of or encountered previously.

I am grateful to John Martino of The Catholic University of America Press for inviting me to write this book, and I hope it will bless the church. Thanks also to Fr. Rob Krol, SJ, Fr. John Mayo, Fr. Paul Hoesing, and Fr. John Horn, SJ, who read earlier versions of this book.

Dcn. James Keating, PhD

Kenrick Glennon Seminary, St Louis, MO
Feast of the Epiphany 2024

One

Developing the Vulnerable
Heart of the Catholic Man

The spiritual life of those in seminary occupies the integrating center of their priestly ministry. Without a seminarian's dedication to prayer, the very moral and psychological core of his being is threatened. Why dedicate one's life of celibacy and ministry to commune with the Spirit of God and then choose to let this communication disintegrate? Time needed to secure an interior life of prayer is one of the key reasons the Church demands years of formation before the celibate state is entered. Such a state in life is entered as a testimony to the reality that God lives and loves. So alive does He become, in fact, that a man can surrender his whole life to Him who is Spirit and find in that surrender his vocation. To live as a cleric without a vital interior life leaves a man in a state of meaninglessness. Such an incomprehensible life drives a priest to create an idiosyncratic

2 · The Spiritual Formation of Seminarians

understanding of his vocation. He ministers simply to secure a living wage, or he demotes sacred ministry to the routinized oversight of rituals and administrative duties, or he finds fulfillment in serving others. One can sense the desperation in such reductionist living. The man has lost his way. He has lost his connection to a loving relationship with God, the very substance of his celibacy.

Along with having a spiritual life, and just as vital for him, is a seminarian's advance in moral and emotional maturity. Such maturity enables the man to receive the gift of stable intimacy with God and share its fruits in pastoral charity. Divine love can best be received into a heart capable of being fascinated with something beyond its immediate needs and wants. One receives this capacity when he welcomes the simultaneous action of grace and truth into his heart, bringing both consolation and challenge. Such conversion is mediated within the relationships we identify as a seminary. Priestly formation prepares a man's heart for communion with God—a communion that will define his life after ordination—and a communion with the people he serves in the parish.

The Apostolic Exhortation *Pastores dabo vobis*, promulgated by Pope Saint John Paul II in 1992, was a major gift to those who minister in priestly formation. Most fundamentally, it was an encouragement to all involved in priestly formation to take seriously the *human* context of spiritual formation. It is that human

Developing the Vulnerable Heart · 3

formation that supports and promotes the relational identity of the priest, both as a man of prayer and of ministry. The document expresses this relational identity in terms of "communion ecclesiology":

> The nature and mission of the ministerial priesthood cannot be defined except through this multiple and rich interconnection of relationships which arise from the Blessed Trinity and are prolonged in the communion of the Church, as a sign and instrument of Christ, of communion with God and of the unity of all humanity.[1]

The priest is specifically in communion with Christ and His own sacrifice upon the cross. Within this communion, "The priest finds the full truth of his identity in being a derivation, a specific participation in and continuation of Christ himself, the one high priest of the new and eternal covenant."[2] This configuration to Christ serves as an anchor for the identity of the whole Church, which is known as the "new priestly people" and which also "receives from him [Christ] a real ontological share in his one eternal priesthood."[3] Thanks to their

---

1 Pope John Paul II, Post-Synodal Apostolic Exhortation *Pastores dabo vobis* (March 25, 1992), no. 12.

2 *Pastores dabo vobis*, no. 12.

3 *Pastores dabo vobis*, no. 13.

4 · The Spiritual Formation of Seminarians

sharing in Christ's mission and authority, "priests are called to prolong the presence of Christ, the one high priest, embodying his way of life and making him visible in the midst of the flock entrusted to their care."[4]

Maturing the Man

While the power of God Himself is fundamental to this mission, the Church insists that the humanity of the priest is instrumental to its success. *Pastores dabo vobis* instructs, "In order that his ministry may be humanly as credible and acceptable as possible, it is important that the priest should mold his human personality in such a way that it becomes a bridge and not an obstacle for others in their meeting with Jesus Christ the Redeemer of humanity."[5] "Of special importance" in this renewed humanity of the priest "is the capacity to relate to others. This is truly fundamental for a person who is called to be responsible for a spiritual community and to be a 'man of communion.'"[6] Unfortunately, due to many causes within a man's own family of origin, within the larger Western culture, and within the subcultures that boys and adolescents inhabit, the seminarian may enter formation with a stunted capacity for communion with God, others, and himself. His own soul may have grown blind to noticing the coping habits

---

4 *Pastores dabo vobis*, no. 15.

5 *Pastores dabo vobis*, no. 43.

6 *Pastores dabo vobis*, no. 43.

Developing the Vulnerable Heart • 5

he developed to assist him with the pain of any emotional (and even physical) isolation. So habitual may this isolation be, and its accompanying coping skills, that the man may be confused about his level of discipleship, believing that he is further down the road to self-forgetfulness than is objectively true. He may be, in fact, still a boy, still affectively immature. John Paul II writes:

> Affective maturity ... requires a clear and strong training in freedom ... to fight and overcome the different forms of selfishness and individualism.... The candidate ... should [also] become accustomed to listening to the voice of God, who speaks to him in his heart, and to adhere with love and constancy to his will.[7]

Hans Urs von Balthasar has noted this same connection between listening (obedience) to God and emotional and spiritual maturation: "The more like young children we are in opening our hearts to this source (which is God Himself) *to receive* its riches, the more grown up and adult we shall be in opening our hearts *to give* to the world and its needs."[8] This paradox of maturity birthed through childlike vulnerability and trust is an essential guiding viewpoint for seminary formators as they listen

---

7 *Pastores dabo vobis*, no. 44.

8 Hans Urs von Balthasar, *Engagement with God* (Ignatius Press, 2008), 49, emphasis added.

6 · The Spiritual Formation of Seminarians

to the life testimony of each seminarian. The Lord wills to meet the men in their "weak" places, those areas of affect or intellect that carry ingrained temptations to isolate from God's love. These places can be characterized by monologues about personal failures, goals unmet or missed, character faults, judgments against the self, and so on. Further, a man can isolate himself from God's love through perfectionistic striving. This habit carries a refrain running through a man's heart: "I am a seminarian; I should be further along in virtue or pastoral competency." Believing that this chorus carries the truth, he begins, in isolation from God, to work really hard at fixing his imperfections. The result, of course, is that his emotional isolation is compounded, and his success at becoming perfect is predictably meager, as Christ warned: "Without me you can do nothing" (Jn 15:5).[9]

If the man opens these places of weakness to God from the beginning, he will find that the holy communion gifted to him will aid in healing any affective or vicious weaknesses more securely than his isolated efforts to perfect himself. In remaining with God in all areas of his life, he becomes more equipped to accept that he has limits to his intellect or virtue or personality. It is common for seminarians to think they must condemn themselves for their sins or failures before the mercy of God can be bestowed. It is a great gift to see them move

---

9 Unless otherwise noted, all Scripture quotations come from the New American Bible.

Developing the Vulnerable Heart · 7

from this lie and begin to live more freely within a life of repentance (Lk 13:3) and not self-hate as prerequisite for divine mercy.

Priestly formation is a journey of healing. Pope Benedict XVI called Christianity itself a therapeutic religion, noting that healing is an essential part of the apostolic mission.[10] Many men enter seminary aware (at least somewhat aware) of their emotional, spiritual, and intellectual weaknesses. If the seminarian expects his formators to fix these weaknesses for him, he needs to be redirected. Formation wishes to introduce the seminarian to Christ as Healer and ultimately, Bridegroom of the Soul.[11] There must first be healing, however, before union with God can be known in its peaceful and sustained communion. To facilitate any needed healing, the director invites seminarians to bring all to God, to pour out their hearts to Him (Ps 62:9). In such faith-filled vulnerability, the man can expect a healing of memories or a thinning out of ideological prejudice or a renewed trust in reason or a movement toward forgiveness of his dad or others, and so forth.

At the same time, we need to prepare a man to embrace the truth that his burdens, faults, and sins do not exhaust his relationship with God. If he imagines

---

10 Pope Benedict XVI, *Jesus of Nazareth: From the Baptism in the Jordan to the Transfiguration* (Doubleday, 2007), 176.

11 St. Bernard of Clairvaux, Sermon 31 in his *Commentary on the Song of Songs.*

8 · The Spiritual Formation of Seminarians

God only as the One to whom he goes wounded and limping, what happens to his prayer once these maladies are relieved or actually healed? He may be confused when he attains a prayer life that is peaceful, indicative of communion. He may sense that prayer is now without a "project," without a "goal." A seminarian may say, "I feel emotionally healed; my anxiety is lessened; I have forgiven my father; I possess a new relationship to my studies or pastoral assignment; now, what is prayer's project?" Here, the director rejoices in his heart that such consciousness has been attained and explores with the man the fuller purpose of prayer: to rest in communion with the One you love. Such a prayer is not a project to complete but simply the man's vocation.

Normally, however, upon entry into the seminary, a man is more in need of the Divine Physician than he is familiar with the peace imparted by the Bridegroom of the Soul. The director assists the seminarian to notice his own emotional and spiritual wounds and encourages him to present them to proper sources of healing: formational, sacramental, and therapeutic. The end goal is a priest capable of leading others into worship, as he first learned to worship rightly himself. One of the fruits of a man entering seminary relationships is his finding assistance in identifying the obstructions within himself that prevent full and free worship of God. Courageously recognizing such obstructions and seeking healing for them prepares a seminarian to be a conduit and not an "obstacle" to the salvation of others.

Developing the Vulnerable Heart · 9

Every man enters priesthood under the influence of God the Father's call, but he enters seminary as one already formed by a variety of factors, both good and bad. This formation (or malformation) must be claimed by the man so he can discern which formation sources should continue and deepen and which sources need to be renounced and their effects emotionally healed. Seminary formators must help seminarians investigate their own lives and to ask themselves: "What have been the sources of formation influencing me until my time of admission to seminary? What has been the effect of these sources upon my interior life and identity?" Armed with such knowledge, formators will be able to assist a man in freeing himself from any negative influences that have entered his heart, healing them where needed. Formators will invite him to reject these sources when evil or untrue and lead him to affirm and build upon them when they are sources of grace.

We can see here that Pope Francis's metaphor for the Church as a field hospital has merit for seminary use as well.[12] Obviously, the seminary aims to avoid accepting men with psychological pathologies, but even emotionally mature men have been influenced by other wounding realities, such as cultural voices promoting the

---

12 Antonio Spadaro, SJ, "A Big Heart Open to God: An Interview with Pope Francis," *America Magazine* (September 30, 2013), https://www.americamagazine.org/faith/2013/09/30/big-heart-open-god-interview-pope-francis.

10 • The Spiritual Formation of Seminarians

dictatorship of relativism, political ideology, and moral license. David Fagerberg describes the condition of many of these men who enter clerical formation: "In our sinful state we direct our life outward toward things that dazzle us now … We are distracted by superficial outer noises because in the Fall we have gone deaf to celestial voices. We mistakenly conclude that the world outside of us is more important than the world within us."[13] Like the Desert Fathers who withdrew from the world but found the echoes of the world still at war within themselves, the relatively controlled environment of the seminary does not in itself root out this underlying condition. It is therefore also legitimate to see the seminary itself as a "battlefield" where the men learn to confront evil and not acquiesce to be victims of dark powers, but instead live in the power of the resurrection.[14]

Acquiring or re-acquiring the capacity to attend to "celestial voices" is constitutive to seminary formation and its purposes. It is common for men coming into the early stages of formation to possess an interior life influenced by "superficial voices" in culture, due in some way to the absence of or rejection of guidance in the ways of spiritual and moral realities. The hold of such superficial formation sources upon men aspiring to the

---

13 David Fagerberg, *Liturgical Mysticism* (Emmaus Academic, 2019), 35.

14 Gratitude to Dr. Anthony Lilles for a conversation bearing insight into this aspect of formation as well.

priesthood may have given rise to John Paul II's call to place the development of affective maturity near the core of seminary formation, as well as the Vatican's more recent call for a universal "propaedeutic" year to precede intellectual formation.[15] Such a call ignites questions in formators' imaginations: How can such maturity be reached within the seminary?[16] How can seminarians advance in the ways of self-donation to God and others?

The answers to these questions are given within the relationships that constitute a seminary. The relationships themselves—with God, formators, peers, and apostolic postings—when lived honestly, support the suffering needed to move a man beyond fascination with half-truths and self-care and finally become fascinated with God and empathetic toward others.

Becoming a Free Man

Seminary, thus understood as a set of relationships, exists in part to facilitate a man's affective and spiritual maturity. Such facilitation is achieved by seminarians

---

15 *Pastores dabo vobis*, no. 43; United States Conference of Catholic Bishops, *Program of Priestly Formation*, 6th ed. (USCCB, 2022), no. 119–20.

16 See James Keating, ed. *A Positive and Stable Masculine Identity: Directions in the Formation of Seminarians* (IPF Publications, 2021); Edward J. McCormack, *A Guide to Formation Advising for Seminary Faculty: Accompaniment, Participation, and Evaluation* (The Catholic University of America Press, 2020).

12 · The Spiritual Formation of Seminarians

truly engaging the areas of formation first articulated by John Paul II in *Pastores dabo vobis*: human, spiritual, intellectual, and pastoral. The internalized integration within the seminarian himself of these four areas of a faith-filled human life measures his progress toward affective and spiritual maturity. This maturity is gifted to the man by way of his personal suffering of and receptivity to the gift of conversion carried by truth and grace. When living a relationship with God in prayer, he can embrace any affective suffering caused by seeing his own disordered status before truth and holiness. When he accepts the reality of needing Christ's healing, a seminarian can then seek the courage to become a patient of salvation. That is, he consents to undergo the unconditional love of God as it salves his own moral and emotional afflictions. In acknowledging that he carries wounds that attract the love of God and that do not repel Him, the seminarian sets off on a journey of discipleship and deeper configuration to Christ.

Entering the suffering of conversion attests to a seminarian's participation in the formative relationships that are seminary. The absence of conversion—and its consequent suffering—indicates a man's presence in formation as self-defined and self-serving. No one is configured to Christ the Priest without first renouncing the areas of life one has given over to idolatry. It is these areas, still in need of the salve of spiritual and moral healing, that keep calling out to each man, "Do you think

Developing the Vulnerable Heart · 13

you can live without us?"[17] As such, it is these areas that entrap a man in a life of nostalgia for sin and afflicted emotions. This nostalgia keeps a man a boy. He remains ensnared in the habits of immediate self-consolation. Wherever the boyish ego is sacrificed and affectivity is exposed to truth, the spousal identity of self-donation can begin to emerge and be embraced. Embracing this spousal self-donation, as opposed to clinging to sin and psychological habit, hastens the time when the seminarian can become configured to Christ the Bridegroom. Sister Gill Goulding observes:

> To give without reserve from a disposition of active receptivity is at the heart of conversion. This leads to a willingness to embrace the cross and "Christ himself becomes the norm that dwells in a new way within his followers without their ever being able to control it." Christ came to suffer with us, not abolish suffering.... [T]rue freedom for human persons is defined by always being indebted to God.... we discover God by obeying him, our fellow human beings by serving them, and ourselves ... in such service and obedience.[18]

---

17 St. Augustine, *Confessions*, Book 8, no. 26.

18 Gill Goulding, CJ, "Holiness of Mind and Heart: The Dynamic Imperative of Conversion and Contemplation for the Study of Theology," in *Entering into the Mind of Christ: The*

14 · The Spiritual Formation of Seminarians

Seminary formation endeavors to help men identify where they resist giving to others without reserve, what sin orders this resistance, and how this resistance can be overcome through repentance. This process of having seminarians identify resistances to spiritual and moral growth and noticing emotional wounds, long denied through coping habits, serves to negate the sins that such hidden wounds birth. Priesthood can be bestowed only upon a free man. Men are truly free to become priests when they become vulnerable to the Holy Spirit's interior searching. The Spirit will recall the wounds and invite the men to repentance where needed.

The true priest-theologian is one who desires and becomes capable of deep contemplative prayer. What I mean by a priest-theologian is a priest who knows God by experiencing Him in prayer.[19] Such prayer is also the life of a true celibate. Contemplative prayer inhabits a man who has finally seen the beauty of God and now desires to be wedded to it. To seek spousal union with the Most Holy Trinity, as all dedicated celibates do, is to desire the very end and purpose of human life. In this way, human formation is foundational to spiritual formation, John Paul II can say, "Human formation, when it is carried out in the context of an anthropology

---

True Nature of Theology, ed. James Keating (Institute for Priestly Formation, 2014), 106.

19 See Adam Cooper, *Holy Eros: A Liturgical Theology of the Body* (Angelico Press, 2014), 3–6.

Developing the Vulnerable Heart · 15

which is open to the full truth regarding the human person, leads to and finds its completion in spiritual formation."[20] Or, as Hans Urs von Balthasar has articulated this same truth, "The man who concentrates on himself in the attempt to know himself better and thus, perhaps, to undertake some moral improvement, will certainly never encounter God.... But if he earnestly seeks God's will in his work, he will—realize himself and find himself."[21]

The seminarian must be formed in "the full truth regarding the human person." In a real way, the early years of formation seek to lead a seminarian in the truth of these questions: What is a man? What is a Catholic? What is a Catholic man (*vir catholicus*)? Here, formation serves to eliminate any partisan bias or emotional affliction that a seminarian might have upon entering seminary. More than ever, the priest must be the bearer of a Catholic anthropology, transcending the secular reductionism of the partisan left or the idiosyncratic devotionalism of the right. By entering seminary life contemplating what a Catholic man is, the seminarian immerses himself in the very remedy capable of healing wounds inflicted upon his soul by contemporary Western culture. Having his eyes opened to the full truth that humans are meant to worship and adore God—that they are ordered toward the transcendent—establishes in him an orientation toward

---

20 *Pastores dabo vobis*, no. 45.

21 Hans Urs von Balthasar, *Prayer* (Ignatius Press, 1986), 115.

16 · The Spiritual Formation of Seminarians

priestly ministry. Human beings are cosmic priests (1 Pt 2:9). "God created everything for man, but man in turn was created to serve and love God and to offer all creation back to him."[22] As formation expands and deepens in him, any trace of partisan thinking can be more readily noticed and jettisoned; any emotional wounds can be healed by his immersion in the full breadth of the spiritual, theological, and human therapeutics offered to him. As he is formed in mature habits of virtue and ponders the meaning of human life before God, he enters a remote preparation for respecting the dignity of those to whom he will be sent in ministry.

The goal of seminary human formation is to gift the Church with a mature and unbiased man, one who has diminished interest in himself. What do I mean by this? Due to original sin, the interest a man has *in himself* is consciously dominant within him.[23] Only committed involvement in sacramental worship and all manner of purification and asceticism by the seminarian (commensurate with his own emotional capacities) will begin to heal this stubborn congenital default setting. I have often pondered Paul Griffiths's comment that for a Christian, there is no "leisure" if by that we mean time for the self in a narcissistic way:

---

22 *Catechism of the Catholic Church* (USCCB Publishing, 2000), no. 358.

23 *Catechism*, no. 390.

St. Benedict's command, *ora et labora,* has [it] right. Work is the temporary remedy for the damage done by the Fall; and worship (prayer) our only anticipation of and proleptic participation in life eternal. Neither is leisured. Both are relational. Neither is narcissistic. Both divert narcissism's self-fascination outward into other-directed action.[24]

With the new *Ratio*'s call for a reimagined seminary formation, it is heartening to see that manual labor is making its way back into seminary schedules.[25] This work with one's hands aids in banishing any thought that one's celibacy is about "navel gazing" or "cloud sitting." Manual labor can give men an integral human satisfaction that

---

24 Paul Griffiths, "Ora et Labora: Christians Don't Need Leisure," *Church Life Journal* (July 18, 2018); cf. Josef Pieper, *Leisure: The Basis of Culture* (Ignatius Press, 2009), who reflects that at the heart of true leisure is festivity, in the sense that life is worship and gratitude to God and, thus, culture is born. Without true worship, we end up worshipping work or entertainment or technological advancements. Thus, we fail to save our culture.

25 Fr. John Floeder, "Propaedeutic Formation Program: Main Feature" (2023). St. Paul Seminary MN, Internal document. "There will also be the regular expectation of manual labor ... including work on nearby farms and rural land." See also Dom Rembert Sorg, OSB, *Holy Work: A Theology of Manual Labor* (Pio Decima Press, 1952) especially Chapter One.

18 · The Spiritual Formation of Seminarians

includes the celibate life as intellectual but not reduced to it. And further, without a true embodied spirituality, celibacy too can be twisted simply into an ecclesial way of bachelorhood. What is beneficial about manual labor is that it is an expression of charity; what the body labors over can be shared with those in need.

As a result of being called to other-directed relationality, the seminarian proceeds along the way of diminished self-interest and becomes awakened to or renewed in a fascination with God, thus preparing him to meet the spiritual needs of others. The seminary aids in completing, therefore, the sacramental journey of moral purification and identity formation begun by family and the pastoral settings of his earlier life. In this way, the seminary assists in securing the seminarian's stable habitation "with Christ" (Col 3:3).[26] In living from this

---

26 "To understand [identity] better, we can return to another Lucan parable on origins, that of the afore-mentioned Prodigal Son in Lk 15:11–32. The younger son goes away from the father to a far country, with the father's property (the paternal *ousia*) now given as the son's own. This filial inheritance is manipulated by the son into a means of refusal of paternal origins; he is not his father's son but his own man. Likewise, I can take my paternally given intelligence, my will, my body, my generated ideas, and narratives, like so many iron filings gathered in a sack, and leave behind the identity-magnet of mission, the logos that orders them. Thus, I make of them my property or *ousia*, to be used to make myself out of myself (Locke ... and Freud). I am from nowhere; this is now my story. And without the magnet of

place that is "above" (Col 3:1), he finds the freedom for which Christ has set us free (Gal 5:1).

Becoming a Man of Worship in Spirit and Truth

In a real way, the relationships within seminary move a cooperating man to live permanently in a liturgical state. That is the goal of formation: to install a man in his new domicile: "For you have died, and your life is hidden with Christ in God" (Col 3:3). This hidden home is the liturgy, the actions of Christ, who, sent from the Father, brings "the many" into communion with Him through the Holy Spirit. Yes, the priest truly lives in the actions of Christ. And all the components of seminary conspire to affect this new permanent dwelling place. To become a priest, one leaves self-interest behind by contemplating and participating in the mystery of the Eucharist. "[Seminary] spiritual formation is first and foremost a participation in public worship of the Church that is itself a participation

---

mission, my gifts may be ordered in any way I like, because they are perfectly fluid on their own. Yet without the ordering logos that comes from outside me, I will (the parable tells me) in fact disperse myself. I will try, like Narcissus, to feed myself from my own image in the pool, not understanding that my imago-nature derives from and reflects the triune God, not myself—and I will, like Narcissus and the Prodigal Son, starve on such empty husks." Angela Franks, "Identity and the Trinitarian Imago," Academy of Catholic Theology Annual Meeting (May 23–25, 2023), 27–28 in original typescript.

20 • The Spiritual Formation of Seminarians

in the heavenly liturgy offered by Christ, our great High Priest.... In the Eucharistic sacrifice, the seminarian learns to offer himself with Christ to the Father and receives spiritual sustenance, Christ's own Flesh and Blood."[27] The relationships and rituals that make up the seminary exist to invite each man into the mystery of the life, death, and resurrection of Christ and hold this mystery as His deepest love and most enlivening commitment.[28] If accepted, this invitation will regenerate the seminarian's faith, hope, and love.

The healing of a man from the inflicted wounds of popular, political, economic, or domestic culture—or simply from his own selfish choices—progresses effectively as the seminarian gives himself over to all the therapeutic formation sources: spiritual direction, counseling, worship, the study of theology itself, friendships, and pastoral assignments. These sources have no power to heal in themselves, however. A seminarian is healed only if he generously participates in the sources *with a vulnerable heart* absent any private agenda.

Developing this vulnerable heart is vital for the seminarian, or all the labor of the formation team will be in vain. History has proven that some men remain in

---

27 *Program of Priestly Formation*, 6th ed. (2022), no. 229a.

28 Fagerberg, *Liturgical Mysticism*, 15. Here, Fagerberg discusses how the Eucharist generates the Church; obviously, what the Eucharist is generating is the spiritual life of the Church's members—most emphatically, its priest members.

Developing the Vulnerable Heart · 21

seminary with impenetrable affect, avoiding vulnerability and fashioning a presence of outward conformity, of precise and anxious role-playing, to hide their character and true motives for seeking a celibate clerical life. Such men were never present as persons but as shape-shifters, regularly discerning the best way to hide truth rather than reveal it and be formed by it. They cling to their own goal of priesthood with all their might, never considering the possibility that they were not even called by God to ecclesial celibacy—but they chose it for their own private and personal motives. Such men will always be found in small numbers among the ranks of those entering the priesthood because the admissions and formation processes are human, administered by broken and fallible humans all along the way. We can only hope that through prayer and prudence, bishops choose their best priests—intelligent, holy priests—to administer formation programs. The presence of those kind of men administering a seminary carries the best hope for the Church that any shape-shifters will be few and far between.When men allow the Lord to shape their character, by contrast, the heart becomes vulnerable to allowing the beauty of the Paschal Mystery to affect it; in other words, these men fall in love with the Most Holy Trinity and place their whole person before God in prayer, revealing their emotional and moral wounds to Him for healing. They discuss these same wounds as appropriate in every forum of seminary life: human formation, spiritual direction, the Sacrament of Reconciliation, and psychological counseling. They pour out their hearts before God in eucharistic adoration and in *lectio divina*. These men, vulnerable men, truly want formation, and they entrust themselves to the Church to assist in their discernment of a priestly vocation. When this discernment is complete, they are ever ready to deepen their appropriation of an authentic, chaste, and celibate priestly vocation.

The Church should only invite men into celibacy who are willing to suffer the coming to life of a well-ordered affect, those who eschew what Dietrich von Hildebrand called "the atrophied heart." The atrophied heart is possessed by those men who refuse to suffer their own spiritual, intellectual, and moral conversion. The extent to which they refuse to suffer the birthing of a new heart is also the extent to which they will make their future parishioners suffer (Heb 10:22). Their unhealed pain will cause suffering in the lives of parishioners who freely and trustingly live under a priest's spiritual leadership. The following description of the "heart" by von Hildebrand can serve as a guide to seminary formators who desire their men to be moved by the Paschal Mystery and, so, refuse to remain in emotional pain out of fear:

> We can readily see the unfortunate neutralization and crippling of the personality which this affective atrophy entails. Those people do not really live who can neither love nor experience a real joy, who have no tears for things that call for tears, and who do not know what genuine longing is, whose

Developing the Vulnerable Heart · 23

> knowledge, even, is deprived of all depth and of any real contact with the object. They are barred from all contemplation; they are cut off from real life, from all the mysteries of the cosmos.[29]

For our purposes, we can understand Hildebrand's reference to the "object" as a seminarian's love of God and his empathy toward the needs of parishioners. For men who suffer an atrophied affect, their heart does not land on an object. They do not rest in a peaceful communion with God or know any interior consolation by serving the needs of others. Instead, they are restless, curious, and superficial in their pursuits. They have their own interests and see them as the most salient object of attention. They are, in other words, affectively immature.

Instead, the Church wants well-ordered men, virtuous men who really desire to live the priesthood, who really want holiness. Such men diminish their own *interests*, but this serves only to enlarge their *hearts*. As Hildebrand says, "Affectivity can never be too intense as long as the cooperation of heart, will and intellect willed by God is not disturbed. In a man in whom the loving, value-responding center has victoriously overcome pride and concupiscence, affectivity could never be too great."[30]

---

29 Dietrich von Hildebrand, *The Heart: An Analysis of Human and Divine Affectivity* (St. Augustine Press, 2007), 56.

30 Hildebrand, *The Heart*, 54.

24 • The Spiritual Formation of Seminarians

What seminary formators are looking for are men of integrity, men who "want but are not a collection of wants."[31] One of the powerful agents to bring about such integrity is an ever-maturing contemplative prayer. Formators propose a holistic, liturgically embedded prayer life as nourishing to the still-developing vulnerable heart. This contemplation is a commitment to behold in love the beauty of God's revealed heart in His only Son, Christ. In such prayer, the seminarian's desire comes to rest upon a substantial reality. This substantial beauty calls out goodness in the contemplative. Beauty calling out goodness in a man is captured by a Greek term, *kallos*. A man who allows beauty to wound his heart will, in turn, be moved to suffer a conversion. This conversion establishes him as a moral presence among others. Prayer concentrated on the mysteries of Christ, therefore, has the power, in part, to call forth a desire in the seminarian to become integrated, mature, and self-donative. Beauty, when truly contemplated, elicits self-gift in the beholder. In contrast, when one only glances at beauty, it can become an opportunity to weigh and measure its usefulness to the viewer, thus setting up an occasion to reduce beauty to a servant of the observer. Whether the beauty is God or a woman, the authentic man stands before it, ready to serve it and sacrifice himself to the truth that beauty carries within it.

---

31 Hildebrand, *The Heart*, 102.

Conclusion

True maturation is accompanied by a disgust for the ways of superficial self-interest. The mature man wants more than self-satisfaction. He wants to forget the self and be taken up into the adventure of self-donative love, even in its sacrificial (that is, priestly) elements. When the seminarian allows his heart to focus on the source of divine love revealed—the Paschal Mystery—this heart becomes anchored in reality. Living in reality allows all the areas of formation to have their influence upon the seminarian's heart. Paying attention to such a substantive object as God, the heart opens, and a sustained life of vulnerability can begin. This is a life opposed to the atrophied heart.

This "wounding" by divine love engenders desire and allows God to reach him and call the seminarian "away from himself."[32] This affectively maturing man, then, simultaneously experiences a hunger for contemplation.

> When men have a longing so great that it surpasses human nature and eagerly desire and are able to accomplish things beyond human thought, it is the Bridegroom Christ who has smitten them with this longing. It is he who has sent a ray of his beauty into their eyes. The greatness of the

---

32 Louis Bouyer, *The Christian Mystery: From Pagan Myth to Christian Mysticism* (Saint Bede Abbey Press, 1990), 279.

26 • The Spiritual Formation of Seminarians

> wound already shows the arrow which has struck
> home, the longing indicates who has inflicted the
> wound.[33]

This "longing" is what the spiritual director searches for within a man's prayer testimony. He invites the seminarian to notice this "longing so great that it surpasses human nature." If present, such a longing is what characterizes a celibate vocation hospitable to receiving priesthood.

The relationships within seminary are to be ordered to deepen this "longing" or to help seminarians notice this beauty or to name if this beauty is even involved in their desire to be celibate.[34] This vulnerability to the beauty of the mystery of Christ is ecclesial, contemplative, and Trinitarian, and it is ordered toward the embrace of one's true vocation. To behold such beauty in prayer is not a

---

33 Nicholas Cabasilas, *The Life in Christ*, the Second Book, Ex-Monastery Library edition (St. Vladimir's Seminary Press, 1997), 15.

34 Augustine, *Confessions*, Book 10, 27:38: "Late have I loved You, Beauty so ancient and so new"; see also Lawrence Feingold's comment: "[Christ] proceeds from the Father as His perfect consubstantial image, lacking in nothing, and reflecting the Father's splendor. For this reason, the Son is associated with beauty" from "The Role of Beauty in Seminary Formation," in *As a Priest Thinks, So He Is: The Role of Philosophy in Seminary Formation*, ed. Beth Rath McGough and Patricia Pintado-Murphy (IPF Publications 2023), 48.

private devotionalism; it is a spirituality of communion "lived out in practical ways."[35] Ultimately, these practical ways order a man to continue in communion well into the life and ministry of priesthood. Such practical ways of remaining in communion with God include the Eucharist, the Sacrament of Reconciliation, adoration, *lectio* and contemplation before the Blessed Sacrament, the Liturgy of the Hours, and the consciousness examen of St. Ignatius of Loyola (or equivalent). Such a practical priestly spirituality deepens a man's desire to preside at liturgical worship, engage in self-donative ministry, and commit to an ever-deepening communion with the Holy Trinity in contemplation. "Spiritual formation is about forming the heart so that it will interiorize the sentiments and ways of acting of Jesus Christ."[36] One way to describe this priestly spirituality is *eucharistic contemplative intimacy with the Divine unto self-gift*; or more prosaically, a life of prayer leads to, upholds, and commends a priestly ministry of pastoral charity. Seminary spiritual formation seeks to deepen the freedom of the seminarian to be possessed by and to possess God as his deepest desire. From this desire fulfilled (albeit not completely until death) will flow a priestly presence that invites others to seek such fulfillment as well.[37]

---

35 *Program of Priestly Formation*, 6th ed. (2022), no. 227.

36 *Program of Priestly Formation*, 6th ed., 228.

37 See Josef Pieper, *Happiness and Contemplation* (St. Augustine Press, 1998), 97–99.

28 · The Spiritual Formation of Seminarians

Our great ally in calling men to this spirituality of a wounded heart is Mary Immaculate, she whose heart was pierced by a sword (Lk 2:35) and who pondered all her experiences in her heart (Lk 2:19). The following prayer was composed by Fr. Leonce de Grandmaison, SJ (1868–1927), and it begs the Mother of God for a heart no longer wounded by the actions of the others, but rather by the beauty of the Trinity:

> Holy Mary, Mother of God,
>
> Preserve in me the heart of a child, pure and clean like spring water; a simple heart that does not remain absorbed in its own sadness; a loving heart that freely gives with compassion; a faithful and generous heart that neither forgets good nor feels bitterness for any evil.
>
> Give me a sweet and humble heart that loves without asking to be loved in return, happy to lose itself in the heart of others, sacrificing itself in front of your Divine Son; a great and unconquerable heart, which no ingratitude can close and no indifference can tire; a heart tormented by the glory of Christ, pierced by his love with a wound that will not heal until heaven.
>
> Amen.

Two

Initial Observations on Seminarian Prayer

Hear my voice, LORD, when I call;
have mercy on me and answer me.
'Come,' says my heart, 'seek his face';
your face, LORD, do I seek!
...
Wait for the LORD, take courage;
be stouthearted, wait for the LORD!" (Ps 27:7–9; 14)

Seminarians ought to be invited to "wait for the Lord" and simultaneously—in that waiting—to "seek his face." These two dispositions may well make up the center of seminarian spiritual formation regarding personal prayer. This waiting and seeking, of course, is placed within the larger context of the eucharistic liturgy, Liturgy of the

30 • The Spiritual Formation of Seminarians

Hours,[1] *lectio divina*, and the maturing processes of human formation that gift a man during his time in the relationships of formation. One might say the "waiting" (absence of any substantive affective movement) is the painful process of God purifying a man's heart of all expectations learned within a culture of immediate gratification. To become a man of prayer is to suffer the demise of surfing the emotions of distraction as the content of one's interior life. Surrendering the expectation that there will be a continual flow of immediately gratifying emotions in prayer can be disappointing to seminarians. When their emotions are not moved in prayer, many seminarians experience this as God "hiding His face."

If the absence of affective movement in prayer is suffered by the seminarian in isolation from the relationships gifted

---

1 I will not explicitly review the commitment all clerics make to pray the Liturgy of the Hours. But certainly, what I write about *lectio divina* can be applied to that commitment as well. The Liturgy of the Hours—like the eucharistic liturgy itself—has both a public meaning and the need for personal appropriation integrated within it. Growing in the habit of personally appropriating the content of Scripture in *lectio* can serve the duty exercised in praying the Liturgy of the Hours as well. Or as David Fagerberg puts it, "The pious reality of the heart and the ritual reality of the cult are but two movements of the same liturgy." David Fagerberg, *The Liturgical Cosmos: The World Through the Lens of the Liturgy* (Emmaus Academic, 2023), 40. If one wants further reading on the Liturgy of the Hours I would recommend: Timothy Gallagher, *Praying the Liturgy of the Hours: A Personal Journey* (Crossroad, 2014).

Initial Obervations on Seminarian Prayer • 31

to him in seminary, then it may retard his prayer's maturation. Speaking about his experience of daily prayer to his director (and others in the seminary) helps a man to live in the reality of what prayer truly is rather than erroneously conforming it to the ingrained standard that expects instant gratification. The director slowly moves the seminarian to anchor his prayer in faith, not personal satisfaction. If a seminarian's grief and confusion about the nature of prayer—that it is devoid of the speed of the internet—is not revealed to his spiritual director, then prayer may become a time of resentment, rumination, and daydreaming. However, a descent into boredom due to a dearth of emotions in prayer may be a grace for him. "When boredom besets prayer that is built on firm foundations of love of God and neighbor, boredom is a sign that the senses are being led from trying to grasp God as an object to a deep stillness that receives rather than grasps."[2] Staying put in and through the boredom purifies the ego's expectations of entertainment or novelty. Waiting on the Lord means, in a contemporary context, exercising trust in prayer that intimacy with God is more like communion than commotion. "Love is situated beyond emotions, which does not, however, mean that we distrust them. Emotion means the wonderful experience of love through a certain harmony of being. Love, on the other hand, is the very fact of a

---

2 Martin Laird, OSA, *A Sunlit Absence: Silence, Awareness, and Contemplation* (Oxford University Press, 2011), 92.

32 · The Spiritual Formation of Seminarians

communion ... on a level that is more profound than the sphere of our feelings."[3]

When the seminarian commits himself to remaining with the Lord in faith, hope, and love, a communion eventually develops in his heart. This communion is experienced as rest, as sustained and gifted inner peace. But this communion, which I would call the revealed "face of God," only follows after and emerges from the waiting. Aborting prayer prematurely by reading or daydreaming one's way through it can be a way for the seminarian to cope with his grief that prayer does not instantly fulfill his longings. Sometimes disorientation in prayer arises not simply from popular cultural influences but from well-intentioned but untutored spiritual reading, raising the hope that prayer will carry strong affective movements, as in "I am waiting for my levitation or stigmata."

The spiritual director accompanies the man as he suffers the deepening of faith and the lowering of expectations that uninterrupted spiritual consolation is prayer's norm. The seminarian begins to embrace or deepen the truth that "faith is contact with the mystery God."[4] Prayer is a loving act of waiting in the Lord's presence, evoking a personal surrender in faith. This

---

3 Jean Danielou, *Prayer: The Mission of the Church* (Eerdmans, 1996), 12.

4 Pope John Paul II, Encyclical Letter *Redemptoris mater* (March 25, 1987), no. 46.

Initial Obervations on Seminarian Prayer • 33

surrender is embedded in and draws its endurance from the sacramental life. Through an ever-deepening faith, the seminarian is brought into contact with a real person. The future priest needs to know that such a life of prayer militates against his fear that loneliness and celibacy are synonymous. Prayer, although spiritual, is not impersonal. The reality that prayer is personal explains why a seminary is not simply a professional school where God is an object of study. Instead, seminary is a community of faith-filled persons who form men in configuration to Christ so they may come to offer their bodies in Christ through the Spirit to God the Father. Ultimately, this priestly offering facilitates Christ's own sacred body to continue in time through the sacraments.

Seminarians are called into intimate and unceasing union with Christ; they are not summoned to simply master intellectual knowledge about God, however vital that is for pastoral ministry. One may note that intellectual formation is needed today more than ever, since reason itself has vacated the public square in favor of subjectivism, emotivism, and ideological slogans in the service of political power.[5] But, nonetheless, "all real

---

5 "We live today in an age of subjectivism in which we may be tempted to place too much trust in our own personal experience, interpretations, and opinions over claims of objective truth." Mark O'Keefe, OSB, *Learned, Experienced, and Discerning: St. Teresa of Avila and St. John of the Cross on Spiritual Direction* (Liturgical Press, 2020), 58.

progress in [the study of] theology ... has its origin in the eye of love and in its faculty of beholding."[6] This description of theology that highlights study as soaked in prayer truly explicates the approach to study characteristic of seminary. Reasoning in faith—in the presence of the Logos—makes thinking clearer and more accurate, not less so.

To reason in the light of prayer secures the future priest as a true contemplative. He develops into one who beholds the truth in love because he knows that both truth and love are the One to whom he has surrendered his life. Contemplation is not for elites; it is a calling for all who reason and love out of faith. "'The rational principle of the universe [Logos] has revealed itself as Love'.... 'Truth and Love are identical'.... That is why the Christian faith ... is based on the fact that 'love and reason [come] together as the two pillars of reality; true reason is love, and love is true reason. They are in unity the true basis and goal of all reality.'"[7] Spiritual direction is most certainly a work of deepening a man's apprehension of and interest in theology class, and theology

---

6 Joseph Cardinal Ratzinger, *Behold the Pierced One* (Ignatius Press, 1986), 27.

7 Daniel Cardó, *What Does It Mean to Believe? Faith in the Thought of Joseph Ratzinger* (Emmaus Academic, 2020), 60–61, quoting (in translation) Joseph Ratzinger, "Uber Zeitgemabheit und Zeitlosigkeit in der Theologie," *Wort and Warheit* 15 (1960): 180.

Initial Obervations on Seminarian Prayer • 35

class is most certainly the secure anchor for any man entering his interior in search of divine intimacy.

"Contemplative prayer is not so much a stage of prayer as it is a fundamental aspect of all prayer."[8] Prayer is a vulnerable, attentive, loving presence whose sole aim is to place the seminarian in the presence of the Divine, waiting for God's face to be beheld. The symbol of the face of God bespeaks both the ultimate end of prayer—which begins heaven on earth—and its temporal reality, understood as personal communication leading to loving communion. Here is what spiritual directors assist seminarians to do: become men who behold, in love, the mystery of Christ's own self-gift. The seminarian enters a relationship with his spiritual director to enable that seminarian to suffer the end of any suffocating self-interest. The direction given to him moves the seminarian to live in "intimate and unceasing union with the Father through His Son Jesus Christ in the Holy Spirit."[9]

This intimate and unceasing union with Christ comes alive in the seminarian as his faith is nourished in eucharistic worship, study, direction, *lectio divina*, and silent prayer. But the enduring gift a spiritual director gives to his directee is the capacity to behold the Mystery of Christ in love. In sharing this gift with the seminarian,

---

8 Thomas Acklin, OSB, and Boniface Hicks, OSB, *Personal Prayer: A Guide for Receiving the Father's Love* (Emmaus Road Publishing, 2019), xxxii.

9 *Pastores dabo vobis*, no. 45.

36 • The Spiritual Formation of Seminarians

the director prepares a man to find his way back to prayer if the passage of time, ministerial burdens, personal rejection, and varied disappointments and griefs known in parish life swamp a priest's heart. Losing his way spiritually and no longer being nourished on the intimacy born of his love for the Paschal Mystery, and from the sacramental heart of the Church, a priest may well descend into functionalism.[10] Here, he attaches his affect and will to lesser goods within ministry, such as measurable success in administrative goals or affirmation from people for his competency in exercising personal gifts ("You are a good preacher"; "You are a good listener"), goals centered upon warming his ego but not deepening intimate communion with the Holy Trinity, the very communion that is his celibate identity. Pope Francis advises:

> Love Jesus more than anything else, let his love be enough for you, and you will emerge victorious from every crisis and every difficulty. For if Jesus is enough for me, I have no need of great consolations in ministry, or of great pastoral success, or of feeling at the centre of extensive relational networks; if Jesus is enough for me, I have no

---

10 See this resource to grasp this reductionist view of priestly ministry more deeply: Eugene Florea, *The Priest's Communion with Christ: Dispelling Functionalism* (Institute for Priestly Formation, 2018).

Initial Obervations on Seminarian Prayer · 37

need of disordered affections, or of notoriety, or
of having great responsibilities, or of pursuing
a career, or of shining in the eyes of the world,
or of being better than others; if Jesus is enough
for me, I have no need of great material posses-
sions, or of enjoying the seductions of the world,
or of security for my future. If, on the other
hand, I succumb to any of these temptations or
weaknesses, it is because Jesus is not enough for
me and that I lack love.[11]

Developing the faculty of the "eye of love"—beholding
in faith the mystery of God's unveiling in the life, death,
and resurrection of Christ—is a prolonged commitment
over time under the tutelage of the director. This tutelage
consists of gently and persistently encouraging the
seminarian to place his heart in a position to be hospitable to the incoming tide of interior silence. "The heart
of spiritual formation is personal union with Christ,
which is born of, and nourished in, a particular way
by prolonged and silent prayer."[12] The *Ratio fundamentalis* speaks directly about the need for seminarians to

---

11 "Message of the Holy Father Pope Francis Signed by
Cardinal Secretary of State for the Meeting with Seminarians
from France" (January 12, 2023), paragraph 5.

12 Congregation for the Clergy, *Ratio fundamentalis
institutionis sacerdotalis: The Gift of the Priestly Vocation*
(December 8, 2016), no. 102. Hereafter *Ratio fundamentalis*.

38 · The Spiritual Formation of Seminarians

become men of interiority. It leaves no doubt about the value of interiority for the diocesan priest, shattering former resistance to such in the name of pragmatism and pastoral priorities. By 'former resistance' I mean the trajectory I read in the *Program of Priestly Formation* in the last century that emphasized a formation concentrating upon professional standards and ministerial skill sets, not in opposition to interiority but lacking the present vigor and centrality attached to prayer found now in the *Ratio* and the *Program of Priestly Formation* sixth edition.[13] To deny the priority of interiority today for the priest is to claim complete ignorance of current and preceding ecclesial and papal documents on priestly formation.[14] The current *Ratio* adds to this even more

---

13 For example, an emphasis on "professional" development (*Program of Priestly Formation*, 1971 "Part One: Professional formation for the Priesthood") becomes an emphasis on "discipleship" (*Ratio fundamentalis*, 2016, *Program of Priestly Formation*, 6th ed., 6).

14 Pope Benedict XVI: "The priest must above all be a man of prayer. The world in its frenetic activism often loses its direction. Its action and capacities become destructive if they lack the power of prayer, from which come the waters of life that irrigate the arid land." "Chrism Mass" (April 13, 2006), paragraphs 29–30.

"Time spent in direct encounter with God in prayer can rightly be described as the pastoral priority par excellence; it is the soul's breath, without which the priest necessarily remains breathless, deprived of the oxygen ... which he needs if he is to

Initial Obervations on Seminarian Prayer • 39

plainly: "The interior man needs to take special and faithful care of the interior spiritual life, centered principally on communion with Christ through the Mysteries … and nourished by personal prayer and meditation on the inspired Word. In silent prayer, which opens him to an authentic relationship with Christ, the seminarian becomes docile to the Spirit, which gradually molds him in the image of the Master."[15]

Interior silence and contemplation preserve the union one has with the Trinity, whether these are chosen at a particular time each day or as they well up within the soul during daily rounds and are generously welcomed by the seminarian. This visitation is vital, not to be missed. Welcoming silence or prayer amid ordinary duties assists in deepening Trinitarian intimacy. Without instruction, seminarians tend to confine prayer to the chapel; teaching them to notice God visiting them where they are and yielding to such visits becomes a liberating gift for their interior lives. What the seminarian pays attention to, what he beholds with the "eye of love," that he will become; hence, the *Ratio*'s note that seminary's goal is to mold men into the image of the Master. Even as the sacrament of Holy Orders contains the *objective* extension of Christ's own actions in time, a man who

---

allow himself to be sent … as a worker into the Lord's harvest." Pope Benedict XVI, "Address to Clergy," Freising Cathedral, (September 15, 2006), paragraph 27.

15 *Ratio fundamentalis*, no. 42.

40 · The Spiritual Formation of Seminarians

becomes a priest must want to *personally* be configured to the self-donative Christ.

Furthermore, to be a priest is to be a man who wants to ponder the Eucharist. This desire springs from a priest's rightly ordered knowledge of the Eucharist. He knows it to contain God's very commitment to His eternal covenant with mankind. "We might understand the Eucharist as being ... the mystical heart of Christianity, in which God mysteriously comes forth, time and again, from within Himself and draws us into His embrace."[16] Christ, now present in signs and symbols, reaches through the priest to offer Himself to mankind for its salvation. This reaching toward humanity by God beguiles the seminarian (and the priest) as a divine act of beauty, drawing him to surrender his own life in response. The Eucharist is God's unfailing commitment to the salvific needs of humanity.[17] Men in seminary should be full of wonder over their call to become agents of this divine commitment. It would be troubling not to hear in spiritual direction a seminarian's deep and consistent attraction to celebrate the Eucharist as the heart of his vocation. No amount of desire to "help people" or "teach" or "listen to people's problems" can truly single out the

---

16 Joseph Ratzinger, *Pilgrim Fellowship of Faith: The Church as Communion* (Ignatius Press, 2005), 121.

17 See Jonathan Ciraulo, *The Eucharistic Form of God: Hans Urs von Balthasar's Sacramental Theology* (University of Notre Dame Press, 2022), 22.

Initial Obervations on Seminarian Prayer • 41

call to priesthood. Desire to surrender one's body in configuration to the surrendered body of Christ on the altar must be the prime desire to deepen, from which flow all capacities for a lifetime of "helping," "teaching," or "listening." To insist on this is not to promote men into a narrow "cultic" priesthood but to assure the Church that it has pastors who both abide in the Mystery themselves and know how to form their people in it as well.[18] Forming people to be configured to the Eucharist and to bear the fruit of such configuration to all facets of lay and public life—this is what a parish exists to do.

Spiritual Formation Embedded in the Mission of Seminary

Seminary formation has become aware of itself as facilitating a two-fold commitment in the future priest: his commitment to a life of contemplating God within which he will also discern the spiritual needs of his parishioners. "Spiritual formation is directed at nourishing and sustaining communion with God. . . . This intimate relationship forms the heart of the seminarian in that generous and sacrificial

---

18 See David Toups, *Reclaiming Our Priestly Character* (Institute for Priestly Formation, 2008). Chapter 2 of this book contains a very helpful overview of how some in the Church tried to redefine priesthood in a more functional manner by emphasizing a more generic ministerial identity and eschewing references to a sacrificial or cultic priesthood.

love that marks the beginning of pastoral charity."[19] The seminary, established as a set of relationships (human and divine), orders itself in the service of forming men of interiority, self-possession, and generous availability. This service endeavors to heal men with identities derived from external performance, achievements, or fantasies of self-ignited heroism. Men of interiority move differently through society and seek to attain a self-knowledge (capacity to grasp true self) unto a self-revelation (capacity to be known by others) unto a self-donation (capacity to discern needs of others and respond to them).

The call for formation to concentrate on equipping future priests with the deepest resources of interiority is especially needed today because the faith is no longer borne by the culture. When one scans the priestly formation documents of fifty or more years ago, the well-formed priest is described in terms of professionalism and pastoral accompaniment.[20] Over the years

---

19 *Program of Priestly Formation*, 6th ed. (2022), no. 225.

20 National Conference of Catholic Bishops (NCCB), *The Program of Priestly Formation* (NCCB, 1971), no. 11.

In reviewing past Programs for Priestly Formation beginning in 1971, the image of priest favored therein was one of a *professional pastoral presence*; today, in response to cultural transformations, I would indicate that the vision of priesthood has become one of a *healed-mystic-teacher*. The healing needed is emotional and spiritual, stemming from a boy's participation in adolescent culture and its lack of demand for a boy to rise to interior maturity.

Initial Obervations on Seminarian Prayer • 43

of ecclesial thinking on what takes priority in priestly formation, one can see that spirituality, not professional standards, has entered such thinking with more emphasis. Today, one notices that the image of the well-formed priest is mystical, a man possessing an interior adherence to the mysteries of Christ (mystic).[21] This promotion—while salutary in itself—responds to the dissolution of a Western culture that once bore the faith in its habits, symbols, and values. Congruent with this mystic turn,[22]

---

21 "The pastoral care of the faithful demands that a priest have a solid formation and interior maturity.... He is called to act with great interior freedom. Indeed, it is expected of him that, day after day, he will internalise the spirit of the Gospel, thanks to a constant and personal friendship with Christ.... The interior man needs to take special and faithful care of the interior spiritual life, centred principally on communion with Christ through the Mysteries celebrated [liturgically] ... and nourished by personal prayer and meditation on the inspired Word. In silent prayer ... the seminarian becomes docile to the action of the Spirit, which gradually moulds him in the image of the Master." Congregation for Clergy, *Ratio fundamentalis* (2016), no. 41–42.

22 "Priestly formation implies a process of configuration to Christ the Head, Shepherd, Servant and Spouse (Cfr. RFIS, 35), which consists in a mystical identification with the person of Jesus, just as it is presented in the Gospels. This mystical process is a gift from God that will reach fulfillment through priestly ordination and constitutes a formative journey that will remain valid throughout all the ongoing formation. Every mystical gift demands the counterpart of ascetical practice, which is the

as noted above, is an urgent need for intellectual prowess on the part of seminarians to counter the diminished place of reason in culture and repel antagonism toward ecclesial doctrine. "Intellectual formation applies not only to a comprehensive understanding of the mysteries of the Catholic faith, but also to an ability to explain and even defend the reasoning that supports those truths."[23] In a sense, priestly formation today is aimed at producing the mystic teacher.[24] But more completely, considering what we know about male adolescents in the Western culture, we can add a third component of modern seminary formation: its relationships endeavor to heal wounds of addiction to technology and self-involvement.[25]

So, at the conclusion of formation, the seminary wishes to gift the Church with a *healed mystic teacher* who, as a priest, abides in the sacramental mysteries and

---

human effort that follows the gifts of grace." Jorge Carlos Patrón Wong, *Foundations of Priestly Formation*, pg. 5, http://www.clerus.va/content/dam/clerus/Dox/Conference%20-%20Foundations%20of%20Priestly%20Formation.pdf (accessed 9/16/2022).

23 *Program of Priestly Formation*, 6th ed., no. 267.

24 "The first task of intellectual formation is to acquire a personal knowledge of the Lord Jesus Christ, who is the fullness and completion of God's Revelation and the one Teacher." *Program of Priestly Formation*, 6th ed., no. 263.

25 See my "From Fantasy to Contemplation: Seminarians and Formation in a Paschal Imagination," *Nova et Vetera*, English edition 16, no. 2 (2018): 367–76.

Initial Obervations on Seminarian Prayer • 45

internalizes the Word of God unto self-donation. He is a man formed through courage, a fortitude exercised in becoming a man of interiority at the service of others' spiritual and moral needs. Spiritual direction assists with this formation in a very concrete way. It is the hope of the director that the formation process produces a man whose way of life is personal union with God as lived from the liturgy.[26] The priest, thus formed, lives a life in union with God and is capable of repentance when union has been eschewed for immediate gratification. Both capacities—communion and conversion—are marked in the man by the grace he welcomed in formation and welcomes still. This is a lacerating grace that deflates *his own way* (Acts 1:2), and empties it of illusory power, while allowing memory to reorient the priest to welcome *the way* (Jn 14:6), in and through the depths of liturgical living. When a seminarian becomes a contemplative and knows that such a life is an abundant one (Jn 10:10), then his will has been ordered toward availability, toward that object of contemplation that presents itself as the way (Jn 14:6).

We understand, of course, that all advance in prayer is due to Christ's gift of His own life poured into the soul of the seminarian, as the seminarian more deeply inhabits a life from and within the liturgy and sacraments. Prayer is never "his" idea; it is always divine gift. During priestly formation the norm for the seminarian

---

26 Fagerberg, *Liturgical Mysticism*, 26.

46 · The Spiritual Formation of Seminarians

will simply be acquired contemplation.[27] Such prayer is born of a vulnerable heart fastened upon the mysteries of Christ out of love. This type of prayer is sufficient for a life of erotic celibacy: a life that seeks to transcend the ego and rest in the communion of God. Any deepening of such contemplation into mystical experiences or infused contemplation is certainly a possibility in God's generosity, but extraordinary within the developmental status of most seminarians. All prayer is a response to grace, but as one is purified of sin and learns to long for abundant life (Jn 10:10) by way of acquired contemplation, it is certainly possible that the hidden Spirit dwelling within may indeed become the primary person praying in the seminarian's soul. Most fitting for seminarians' formation in prayer is a stress on allowing God to lead in prayer, to privilege listening to God and formators over singular interior experiences, and to substantively ground personal prayer in the Incarnation (*lectio divina*) and in an active participation in the Eucharist.[28]

---

27 Acquired contemplation is born of meditation. This meditation opens the mind to think about the goodness of God, such exposure to His goodness moves the heart to love Him more deeply. This love invites the seminarian to desire time in God's presence as a priority. For more see, Jordan Aumann, *Spiritual Theology* (Bloomsbury, 1980).

28 See Bernard McGinn commenting upon Hans Urs von Balthasar's notion of prayer in *The Foundations of Mysticism: Origins to the Fifth Century* (Crossroad, 1992), 290.

Initial Obervations on Seminarian Prayer • 47

The Listening Needed to Form Healed Mystic Teachers

Seminary spiritual direction is placed at a crucial juncture in the overall set of relationships that make up priestly formation. In this forum, a director and a seminarian delve into that seminarian's current relationship with the Most Holy Trinity. This is usually done by focusing upon the content of his personal prayer in the context of a liturgical and sacramental environment. The priestly formation documents of the Church remind spiritual directors that they "should foster an integration of spiritual formation, human formation, and character development consistent with priestly formation.... [assisting] the seminarian in acquiring the skills of spiritual discernment."[29] Priestly spiritual direction "is directed at nourishing and sustaining communion with God and with our brothers and sisters, in the friendship of Jesus the Good Shepherd.... This intimate relationship forms the heart of the seminarian in that ... sacrificial love that marks the beginning of pastoral charity."[30] The director promotes a life in the seminarian that is ordered "toward intimate and unceasing union with God" in the context of future priestly ministry within the Church.[31]

---

29 *Program of Priestly Formation*, 6th ed., no. 106; see also *Ratio fundamentalis*, no. 107.

30 *Program of Priestly Formation*, 6th ed., no. 225–26.

31 *Program of Priestly Formation*, 6th ed., no. 226–27; *Ratio fundamentalis*, no. 101–2.

48 · The Spiritual Formation of Seminarians

The director, then, holds the "whole man" before him when a direction session begins. Listening to this whole man calls the director to engage in supplication for the gift of integrative intuition. This intuition connects what is being shared in direction by the seminarian with his life as he is living it now, those aspects that he carries from a past boyhood, and his nascent generosity toward letting Christ live His priesthood over again in his body. This kind of intuition can emerge over years of experience in direction but is founded upon a desire in the director to listen for openings to the full truth of a man as these present themselves in each conversation. Who a man is will obviously be revealed progressively. Begging the Holy Spirit for wisdom when such "openings" occur is the standard disposition in all direction sessions. Fundamentally, the director follows these openings to aid a man's vocational discernment. Does what is being revealed indicate the seminarian has the capacity to receive priesthood, or if discernment has matured does he welcome its deepening within certain areas still in need of healing or growth? Is his humanity becoming hospitable to the supernatural? Is he becoming vulnerable to receive the gift of priesthood and give himself away in charity as response to that gift?[32] This capacity to embrace self-donation as vocation is measured by the presence of interior maturity. The *Ratio* observes:

---

32 See *Pastores dabo vobis*, no. 23.

Initial Obervations on Seminarian Prayer · 49

> The pastoral care of the faithful demands that the priest have a solid formation and interior maturity.... He is called to act with great interior freedom. Indeed, it is expected of him that, day after day, he will internalise the spirit of the Gospel, thanks to a constant and personal friendship with Christ.... In contemplating the Lord ... he will be able to give himself generously and with self-sacrifice for the People of God.... [T]he interior man [is] centred principally on communion with Christ through the Mysteries celebrated [liturgically] ... and nourished by personal prayer and meditation on the inspired Word. In silent prayer ... the seminarian becomes docile to the action of the Spirit and ... moulds him in the image of the Master.[33]

The Church will recognize the man who is truly called to priesthood by his surrender to a conversion that internalizes a personal friendship with Christ, embraces contemplation as a source for pastoral charity, chooses an interior life focused upon the Paschal Mystery, and deepens a love for and immersion in interior silence. These character traits will truly identify who in the seminary is surrendering to the process of celibate priestly "molding" and conversely, who is called to another way of holiness.[34]

---

33 *Ratio fundamentalis*, no. 41–42.

34 See *Ratio fundamentalis*, no. 42.

50　•　The Spiritual Formation of Seminarians

This invitation into divine intimacy through a call to connect pastoral ministry with interiority, as stated in the 2016 *Ratio fundamentalis*, may raise some fear within clergy and seminarians. Some may resist such a contemplative description of priesthood; instead, they move to fashion a foundation for pastoral ministry that is more pragmatic and goal oriented. Theirs would be a foundation set upon personal gifts and well-trod avenues of skill sets and organizational competencies. To base priestly ministry upon interior configuration to Christ can seem unimaginable, easily dismissed as so much "poetry." But the spiritual director is charged with keeping future priests in reality: the charge in the *Ratio* is not poetry; it is, instead, to follow Saint Paul, "no one can lay a foundation other than the one that there is, namely, Jesus Christ" (1 Cor 3:11), and the Lord Himself, "everyone who listens to these words of mine but does not act on them will be like a fool who built his house on sand" (Mt 7:26).

Formators should tell seminarians the truth: in today's culture and environment, the priest will face rain falling, floods coming, and winds blowing and buffeting the house. They only need look around to see those whose priesthood has "collapsed" and been "completely ruined" (Mt 7:27) without an interior life. Spiritual formation must gradually awaken the men to the Lord's question, "Which of you wishing to construct a tower does not first sit down and calculate the cost to see if there is enough for its completion?" (Lk 14:28). The cost, as Jesus

Initial Obervations on Seminarian Prayer • 51

makes clear, is to "carry his own cross" (Lk 14:27); even a so-called career as a minister is ultimately a "possession" that must be renounced by a disciple (Lk 14:33). It is the recognition of the morality of a death sentence of sorts— in this case, approval for priestly formation to "kill" the ever-unruly ego, the "old self," the sinful body" (Rom 6:6). The director is charged to ask: Considering this death sentence, do you wish to go forward in priestly formation and become a man of interiority? Do you wish to find your identity in communion with the Holy Trinity, rather than in ministerial "success" and functionality?

Personal Agendas

Emotional and spiritual intimacy with the Holy Trinity is demanding. Those seminarians with unhealed personal agendas will resist such intimacy, wishing to use priestly life to remain self-focused. In formation, this resistance can take the shape of role-playing, external adhesion to "the program" so that later, one can fit priesthood into the life the man really wants to live. Authentic encounter with the living God, of course, dismantles this role-playing, but a man must be humble enough to want to be affected by God. Inviting men into authentic intimacy with God in prayer, teaching them how to receive divine love, and encouraging them to remain in a receptive posture toward such love is the director's contribution to a unified formation process. The director can help to identify such "role-players" and invite them to exit

52 • The Spiritual Formation of Seminarians

formation. If the whole formation team understands and promotes an authentic vision of the *Ratio* and the *Program for Priestly Formation*, it will create a communal environment that makes it difficult for "users" to remain. Such an environment will be overtly evangelical and contemplative. It will not tolerate cynicism among seminarians, nor will it tolerate seminarians who think only in terms of political ideology.

It will also be inhospitable to men who remain focused upon immature "self-care" or who attempt to "enlist" other seminarians in the ways of clericalism, role-playing, or duplicitous living. When these seminarians master the "system," they find quite chillingly that "there is no longer a need to fight against God ... [they can] simply ... do without Him."[35] In these rare (but ecclesially damaging) cases, a man clings not to intimacy with the Trinity as his way of formation but simply to his own way (Acts 1:25). This way is ordered toward domesticating the mystical into the personally expedient and useful. These men are masters at averting their eyes from the supernatural approach of God so they might become ecclesial bureaucrats with eyes on the clock and their travel apps.

In order to alert those who use the seminary for their own ends that such cannot be continued, the director is to inquire about and promote, where it is anemic, a seminarian's internalization of the mysterious yet eminently practical reality of entering and maintaining

---

35 *Pastores dabo vobis*, no. 7.

a "constant and personal friendship with Christ."[36] Such friendship was first promoted in contemporary times within the foundational statement of modern priestly formation at the Second Vatican Council: "The spiritual training should be closely connected with the doctrinal and pastoral, and, with the special help of the spiritual director, should be imparted in such a way that the students might learn to live in an intimate and unceasing union with the Father through His Son Jesus Christ in the Holy Spirit."[37]

Intimacy with God

The thought of beginning a process of intimacy with God is intimidating, even for those without a personal agenda for being in seminary. For those men of "pure heart" who wish simply to be formed as priests, the call for transparency in prayer can begin as a halting experience. Directors know they need to be gentle and invitatory, as they unfold the goals of prayer and share their recommendations with seminarians on how to become vulnerable to the presence of God. Listening to the seminarian unveil his heart, the director notes if it is a heart full of God or simply full of ideas about God. It becomes clear

---

36 *Ratio fundamentalis*, no. 41.

37 Vatican Council II, Decree on Priestly Training *Optatam totius* (October 28, 1965), no. 8; see also *Pastores dabo vobis*, no. 45, and *Program of Priestly Formation*, 6th ed., no. 226.

over a few sessions if this man has suffered some level of ego displacement in prayer and is now beginning to think and choose behavior out of communion with God or if he is still exploring who God is more so through books or other people's testimonies.

No doubt, there are seminarians who already have true contemplative lives, but many remain ignorant of the depth of presence to which God wishes to call them. These men will remain in touch with God through their vocal prayer and vocational discernment to great benefit. They are eager to look to the director for guidance since they have pure hearts and willingly explore how the contemplative aspect can fill all their prayer. They especially look to the director for wisdom as they need to develop the patience to "wait on the Lord." The director is called to encourage a deepened intimacy in the seminarian who glimpses the contemplative dimension of prayer. The "unceasing intimacy" with God highlighted by the ecclesial formation documents may first begin in a seminarian during conversations with his director. Here, he is taught how to remain available to the Holy Spirit during vocal prayer. This availability is vital so that God can awaken within the seminarian an awareness that he is in the presence of a real person. Of course, this deepening and awakening is accomplished in the Spirit by the director's own prayerful attention to each seminarian as an individual. There is no one-size-fits-all approach (as measured by the man's year of formation, for example).

Initial Obervations on Seminarian Prayer • 55

Attaining intimacy with God is both gift and task, and so the director's role is to invite the seminarian to vulnerability in prayer, open to receive divine gifts. At the same time, the director guides him to remain in the presence of God throughout the day. Within this reality of intimacy as *gift-task*, a seminarian can make progress in the "constant personal friendship" with God to which the seminarian is called. To attain intimacy with God, the seminarian enters into the disciplines of both silent receptivity (gift) and conscious self-revelation (task). It is common for seminarians to initially experience prayer as asking God for things, virtues, and experiences and then slowly realize that they have missed the Giver for the gift. They may find that they have received something from God but do not know how to remain with God. In this case, the seminarian continues in a restless loneliness, making celibacy unsustainable.

Many seminarians are like Martha of Bethany (Lk 10:38–42) and remain alone in the kitchen of busy accomplishments while resenting those persons who have chosen "the better part" (Lk 10:42). Such "Marthas" have a hard time choosing presence over accomplishment because they cannot yet see that it is only by remaining with God that their ministrations "bear much fruit" (Jn 15:5). Mostly in innocence and ignorance, the seminarian wants to become perfect, successful on his own. Many men are surprised to find out that they use God to help them live a life of achieved competence without really being with Him. It can be a stinging realization for

56 · The Spiritual Formation of Seminarians

a seminarian to become aware that he is doing this is. The Martha-Mary story is filled with much depth for the men to pray with, as it helps them name the loneliness of self-achievement and the unconscious resentment toward God that goes along with it, and to receive the loving but firm rebuke of the Lord for their attempt to follow him "burdened with much serving" (Lk 10:40). With such knowledge, the Spirit can eventually move a man to the position of Mary, raptly attending to the presence of God.

As the seminarian stops choosing to manage his own affairs, accomplishing goals by the power of his natural abilities, he may experience a bit of identity vertigo. Such emotional unsteadiness indicates he is only just beginning to embrace the truth that ministry (his "accomplishments") flows from communion. It is Christ who fills his ministerial actions with power, an effective power that flows from remaining with Christ. The true end of priestly celibacy, being with the Divine, is what is vital in the cleric's life; and God will distribute the fruit of a man's labors out of that sustained prayer (1 Thes 5:17). When dealing with men who have anxiety issues, for example, directors must be very gentle in suggesting that the men remain with God all through the day. This invitation can otherwise turn into a demand of their wounded conscience to be "always thinking about God." Here, they confuse faith for a false moral demand to conjure up God before their imaginations steadily through the day. So, the director reassures such a man

Initial Obervations on Seminarian Prayer · 57

that such focus upon God is only possible in heaven; here on earth, we do our best to turn to God throughout the day according to our own limits and capacities.

At times, I ask seminarians to meditate imaginatively upon the Martha-Mary story beyond the text's ending. Invariably, many men welcome in prayer the image of Jesus and Mary joining Martha in the kitchen. Here, they sense Martha's growing joy is not gained from receiving help with chores but from finding herself no longer alone in their execution. Such a conclusion shifts a man's heart from thinking prayer and ministry are going to give him things, ideas, experiences that secure his identity to simply embracing an identity that flows from the truth that "God is with us" (Mt 1:23).

This meditation carries with it a hope that a man will remain in the presence of God as best he can, eschewing the temptation to minister alone ever again. It is mysticism—prayer—that moors ministry. If ministry is founded upon anything less, it may emanate not from divine love received but from emotional neediness seeking a resolution. Mysticism is a life penetrated by the mysteries of Christ through prayer and sacramental worship. Such penetration secures a man in his own identity and mission, a life sent from communion, not a life looking for it. Unless the celibate cleric is fascinated with God, ministry can become self-serving. Mature ministry is born of the fruit of communion with the Holy Trinity, a communion deepened within the very practices and relations of seminary formation. Embracing

58 • The Spiritual Formation of Seminarians

this maturity, the seminarian can fall into silent wonder over the simplicity of God's will for him: He wanted to call the seminarian to Himself so that He might be with the seminarian in life and ministry (Mk 3:13–14).

This silent wonder, being receptive to the Divine Presence, orders the seminarian's attention to the Paschal Mystery by way of relational prayer, *lectio divina*, and participation in liturgical rites. Part of the wonder is over the very possibility one has of entering contemplation. This possibility is itself a gift, one bestowed upon believers by the ever-flowing revelation of God's own interior life in Christ. But it is a gift of grace, not a gift bestowed upon spiritual elites. Certainly, one cannot have a steady heart fastened upon the beauty of Christ if mortal sin is still habitually chosen, but a life of virtue is possible if contemplation of God is the object of one's love. As a virtuous vocation celibacy is brought to a man in the same way marriage is brought to a man: from the body of a person. The woman brings marriage to a man from within her very being, a being that both attracts and repels: attracts due to its beauty, but repels due to the hidden call to sacrifice. He will only reconcile these opposite pulls when he learns that his being is fashioned not merely to enjoy the beauty, but to sacrifice for it. In the same way, a man is called to celibacy in the approach of God. Celibacy that is a true call is never about a life of living alone. How could it be, if the only sane reason for choosing it stems from the presence of a Divine Person whose beauty called

Initial Obervations on Seminarian Prayer · 59

one into it? Celibacy and marriage are in this way the same; they are relational. Both are about communion, and both are about sacrifice.

And so, the director says to the seminarian who is disposed to be affected by the Paschal Mystery, "Listen; pay attention; behold what Christ is revealing to the Church and to you personally." Over the course of formation, if the seminarian heeds this guidance, he will become enamored of the object he contemplates. Completing this capacity to behold is the courageous act of the seminarian's own self-revelation to the object of his contemplation. Here, we remind the men that prayer is the safest emotional place on earth, if the seminarian is worshipping the true God and not a distorted image. All that he has to lose is everything about himself that is false and destructive. Such worship of the authentic God is vital for obvious reasons: one cannot effectively reveal oneself to an idol, to a god who holds exaggerated or contrary aspects of the true God, or to a distorted god passed on by other persons' emotional wounds.

In cases where a man recognizes he has been worshipping a distorted image of God, the director may share some doctrinal teaching with the seminarian so it can be incorporated consciously into the man's prayer and the man can progress in discernment. Of course, intellectual errors on the nature of God will be rectified in theology class, but a seminarian may have fastened to a distorted image of God by way of an affective wound or experience, and, so, surrendering those types of distortions will encompass a series of conversations and prayer sessions over the length of the director's relationship with the seminarian. Here also is one of the many occasions a spiritual director would refer his directee to the seminary's psychologist for exploration in affective healing of wounds stemming from family-of-origin issues or possible emotional trauma from another life experience. The combination of prayer and counseling is thus a fruitful integration used by grace to heal many men in formation.

Three

From Loneliness to Solitude to Communion

The term "seminary" means "seed bed"—since the time of St. Charles Borromeo, it has been intended to be a safe, even sheltered place in which the seeds of a vocation can grow into a mature plant able to be replanted in the mission field with all of its storms and droughts. But as I began to discuss last chapter, seminary today is not free of the weeds that the Enemy has sown already in men's lives and continues to plant. Seminaries are a supernatural battle ground where Satan wishes to do one thing: Stop clerics from praying. It was the Desert Father Evagrius who articulated this battle very clearly when he enjoined monks to watch over their thoughts.[1] This watching was a guarding against negative/sinful

---

1 Evagrius, *Praktikos*, in *Praktikos and Chapters on Prayer* (Cistercian Publications, 1981), 6.

62 · The Spiritual Formation of Seminarians

thinking lest the passions become aroused, but it was also an invitation to allow silence the opportunity to yield self-understanding. All of the scheduled prayer times in the world will be no help to the prospective priest (or his formators) without this watching. Satan knows a man's weak points and knows which tempting thoughts or which self-loathing thoughts will be most efficient in shutting down the prayer of any cleric.

This, then, is *the* task of seminarian prayer: Behold the authentic revelation of God; reveal wounds to this unveiled God to know a growing peaceful communion with the presence of such Holy Mercy, and desire and protect prayer as one's very oxygen.[2] Over years, in the interpenetration of the gift and task that is prayer, a seminarian, when assisted by all the components of formation, will become a man of discernment and contemplation. Within this discernment, he will receive his vocation; and if it is to priesthood, he will grow ever more attracted to a life of pastoral charity. "The pastoral care of the faithful demands that a priest have a solid formation and interior maturity."[3] There are few more certain indications of a man's emotional and spiritual maturity than his willingness to suffer the transformation from an externally-bestowed identity (achievements and "success") to an identity secured from a vulnerable receptivity

---

2 See Pope Benedict XVI, "General Audience," Wednesday, May 16, 2012, paragraph 3.

3 *Ratio* (2016), no. 41.

From Loneliness to Solitude to Communion · 63

within himself, that is contemplative prayer, which can then receive the gift of sonship from the Father. The "pastoral care of the faithful demands" such a man of interior maturity because the laity expect the priest to belong to and know God.[4]

Being Loved for Who I Am or What I Do?

Many seminarians deep down believe the stubborn lie that a man's lovability is something he can control, something he can earn. They tend to want to clean up their house first before they allow God to visit, rather than to invite God into the mess and clean it up together. They have a difficult time believing that that the relationship between themselves and God will be secure when God sees their mess. What would frighten them even more is if God chose not to assist them in cleaning and healing and forgiving but simply wanted to "sit in the mess" with them. To have a seminarian pray with this last image is very difficult, as it exposes how deep the "achievement theology" has entered his soul. Seminarians tend to forget that it is being in the presence

---

4 "The faithful expect only one thing from priests: that they be specialists in promoting the encounter between man and God. The priest is not asked to be an expert in economics, construction or politics. He is expected to be an expert in the spiritual life." Pope Benedict XVI, "Meeting with Clergy" (May 25, 2006).

64 · The Spiritual Formation of Seminarians

of the beauty of God that elicits new behavior. If they let God live with them long enough, they will want to clean their room, and they will even do it grace-fully. Their moral behavior will be a response to His own beauty and love; it will not be an effort to win His love. Even if they let God in to help clean the mess, many are shocked to realize that it was still their own agenda being followed. Having God just be with them in the mess—to be loved within such emotional and spiritual chaos—tests their capacity to accept God's way of acting. As evangelical psychologist David G. Brenner observes:

> Receiving love while still trying to earn it will only ... increase [the seminarian's] efforts to earn love.... It is not the fact of being loved unconditionally that is life changing. It is the risky experience of allowing myself to be loved unconditionally.... [W]illingness to receive the love of God ... without earning it is at the heart of both psychological and spiritual growth.... I cannot feel the love of God because I do not dare to accept it unconditionally.[5]

To want to follow God's agenda is to want to know God. Knowing and serving God is certainly the end of seminary spiritual direction, but this comes from gaining

---

5 David G. Benner, *Surrender to Love: Discovering the Heart of Christian Spirituality* (InterVarsity Press, 2015), 74–75.

From Loneliness to Solitude to Communion • 65

the confidence that one is known and accepted by God even before one's efforts. Priests can advise parishioners on the nature of God because of their academic study in seminary. Presenting the true God from the ambo and in the catechetical classroom is a vital and irreplaceable work in the Church. But parishioners also need a spiritual father who loves the Holy Trinity and can help them with their prayer lives because the foundation of his own interior life is the merciful embrace of the Father that is open to all.

A man comes to seminary to explore an attraction to the celibate priesthood. This attraction is one borne to his heart by a Divine Person. This Person wants to be engaged during a man's time in formation. Unfortunately, the horarium of many seminaries can become so packed with daily or weekly duties, it can be lost to a seminarian that formation exists to deepen a relationship with the One who has called him into celibacy. Seminarians new to formation can run themselves into the ground emotionally trying to succeed and achieve and be dutiful, all in the name of being formed in their vocation. Such a habit of going from duty to duty and accomplishment to accomplishment leaves the seminarian in a place of emotional isolation. "I have so much to do." This isolating cry, as in the previous example of the Martha-Mary story, needs to be listened to by directors so that they can guide the man back into the simplicity of communion with Christ. The new prescription of a propaedeutic year in all U.S. seminaries (like the long-standing institution of the novitiate in religious life) is a positive step in mitigating

66 • The Spiritual Formation of Seminarians

this danger, but this mindset can easily creep back in over the succeeding years of increased activity. Further, the director might be a moderating voice of reason to those in charge of the seminary schedule.

The seminarian may even come to interpret his growing academic and pastoral competency as a sign that self-reliance pays off. Being self-reliant may win him an excellent thesis or produce an empathetically executed counseling session at the parish youth group. Self-reliance as such is not affirmed by formation leadership in these instances, but he interprets it as such since formation leadership may praise his results but not have asked him how he composed his academic thesis with the wisdom of the Word or how he effectively listened to a teenager in distress at youth group with grace of the Holy Spirit. Inadvertently, he interprets his success as originating in natural gifts and talents. He is so "smart"; he is so "empathetic." Hence, his myth of self-reliance continues, and a key aspect of celibacy may be left unexplored. Does he like being with God, or does he prefer to do things on his own?

One way a director can guide a man back into communion is to open a new way to approach study, one that rightly orders knowledge as serving love under the influence of faith.[6] The love of God can thus found a

---

6 See these resources for detailed descriptions and rationales for how theology and prayer interpenetrate: James Keating, ed., *Entering into the Mind of Christ: The True Nature of Theology*

From Loneliness to Solitude to Communion · 67

man's studies rather than be in competition with them. To found theology upon such love can yield healing in a seminarian otherwise driven to succeed or stand out. It can also be an ally in the quest to renounce study habits that isolate him from the relationships that are seminary or arise to serve false or egocentric goals. One is not in a seminary to "succeed" at a grade point average but to eventually possess an integrated theological knowledge founded upon God's love and fraternal communion, a love overflowing into pastoral charity. The seminary exists to promote, facilitate, and guard the communion the men have with the one true God and their brothers. To remain in this communion gently guides a man and capacitates him to understand divine love theologically and execute pastorally the love he has received in both prayer and study.

By loving God in prayer, the seminarian begins to adhere to Him who is beauty, goodness, and truth. It is an adherence founded upon theological faith that enflames a desire to communicate himself with God and receive from God His own self-communication. This sacred exchange involves the whole man—hence, the inadequacy

---

(Institute for Priestly Formation, 2014); James Keating, *Resting on the Heart of Christ: The Vocation and Spirituality of the Seminary Theologian* (Institute for Priestly Formation, 2009); David Fagerberg, "Prayer as Theology" in his *The Liturgical Cosmos*, 1–20; Anton Štrukelj, *Kneeling Theology* (The Catholic University of America Press, 2023).

68 · The Spiritual Formation of Seminarians

of reducing prayer simply to discursive thinking or objective reflection.[7] Instead, prayer is a man communicating himself to God in response to being loved by Him.

Desire in Prayer

The long-range result of such self-communication is that this same man becomes a prayer. The commitment to pray becomes an identity to be possessed; one becomes communication with God. Little by little, one becomes holy. In this commitment to prayer, the role of affect is as crucial as the role of reason and will. Affect in prayer is the adhesive that keeps a man attached to God in desire. As so many have cautioned, this does not mean, that prayer can be reduced to emotion or "experiences" of devotion alone.[8] The affective movement in prayer

---

7 "The experience of love at the level of the heart determines … basic human flourishing … as well as the health of the rational faculties and thus both an understanding of and capacity to adhere to reality." Weronika Janczuk, "The Place of the Heart in Integral Human Formation," *Logos* 21, no. 1 (2018): 141. The love needed here at the level of the heart is one received at the level of my own innate goodness, at the level of being. I must experience affirmation of myself at this level—and not simply at the level of my talents or usefulness or successes—to become a whole and freely self-donating human being.

8 "Interpreting emotion as a sign of divine presence can be hard to resist. But feelings in prayer are bound to vary.… When emotion is considered the measure of proximity to God, what

From Loneliness to Solitude to Communion · 69

makes itself known mostly as a state or habit of longing or desire, never a guaranteed indulgence.

Desire is of paramount importance to the process of spiritual formation in seminary. The director is to notice where the seminarian's desires may be guiding him. The director then assists the seminarian to notice these desires as well, guiding the seminarian to dwell in them during his daily Holy Hour. If he has a vocation to the priesthood, this desire should be nuptial. It should be a longing to give himself away at the altar of sacrifice to the Father with Christ the Bridegroom in the Holy Spirit for the sake of His Bride, the Church. This altar is the universal one of spousal love, of complete self-giving. One's body must become an altar configured either in matrimony or celibate self-donation, but both are participations in the one act of Christ giving all as Husband.[9] "The priesthood has no other function than to make transparent the love of Christ for his Church."[10]

---

are we to say of prolonged dry periods of prayer? That God has abandoned us.... The reality of love itself in God simply has depths of mystery that do not allow easy communications." Donald Haggerty, *Contemplative Enigmas: Insights and Aid on the Path to Deeper Prayer* (Ignatius Press, 2020), 114.

9 See the following for the most complete theological meditation on the spousal nature of Christ and the priesthood: Andrew H. Cozzens, *A Living Image of the Bridegroom: The Priesthood and the Evangelical Counsels* (Institute for Priestly Formation, 2020).

10 John Nepil, "A Miracle of Grace: Hans Urs von Balthasar's

Within shared prayer and conversation on the spousal nature of Christ, the director is moving a man into affective maturity, into a life that recognizes an emotionally mature male gives of himself and orders his life around the needs of others. John Paul II writes, "The priest, who welcomes the call to ministry, is in a position to make this a loving choice, as a result of which the Church and souls become his first interest, and with this concrete spirituality he becomes capable of loving the universal Church and that part of it entrusted to him with the deep love of a husband for his wife."[11] To achieve such conformity to Christ, the Chaste Spouse, the priest enters into the great mystery of obedience, of deep and rapt listening to the needs of "the bride," the Church. For the seminarian to become such a priest, he needs to listen deeply in prayer so as to discern if such a way of spousal love is being gifted to him by the Father.[12]

The director helps the seminarian discern what exactly his "first interest" is and whether this fascination carries within it a vocation to celibacy. Of course, we know that before a person's own moral and spiritual conversion, one's "first interest" is usually oneself. To carry oneself as one's own first interest is a great burden

---

Vision of Priestly Spirituality," *Communio: International Catholic Review* 49 (2022): 68.

11 John Paul II, *Pastores dabo vobis*, no. 23.

12 "Obedience is the very nature of the priest," Nepil, "A Miracle of Grace," 69.

From Loneliness to Solitude to Communion · 71

for the emotionally normal seminarian. As his prayer life matures, he gets more and more frustrated that his own interests (passing exams, relating to peers, having authority problems, having pastoral ministry failures, etc.) keep intruding into prayer. He wants to "get over himself," but such complete and pure fascination with God and the needs of others slips away as the will is weak and personal needs seem so urgent. Dying to self-involvement appears to be as difficult as physically dying. Just as there are people who die with a serene passing, there are as many in hospice, fighting and struggling to hold on to one's self. So it is, analogically, in prayer as well. In a real way, seminary spiritual directors are spiritual hospice workers encouraging seminarians to "let go of the self and entrust all to God."

But the analogy with death goes only so far, as the "fat, relentless ego" continues to remain,[13] pulsing its energy even in the deeply committed spousal-celibate seminarian. Hence, the inner peace of the "imperfect" seminarian lies in recognizing the victory is God's despite a man's own return to sin. As Balthasar observed, "the office [of priest] has been able to succeed in him despite his inadequacies.... His gift of self has primarily the form of humility."[14] So the ego, the selfish self, is not extinguished so as to leave only an ego corpse. Rather,

---

13 For example, Iris Murdoch, *The Sovereignty of the Good* (Routledge, 1970), 51. It's a phrase she used often.

14 Nepil, "A Miracle of Grace," 69–70.

spiritual formation produces a humbled self, one that acknowledges personal weaknesses and gifts before the Living God. This humbled self contends with the pulsing energy of the ego remnant (the self-centered drives of our nature) and regularly relates this ego residue to the integrative power of contemplative prayer. In this way, the ego is de-centered and functions less and less as a man's source of action or self-worth.[15] Instead, he slowly moves toward freedom; what a man is before God, that he is and no more. Formation's healing edges a seminarian toward true humility so he can leave behind any false projections of heroism or perfectionism or work-a-holism.

The director's accompaniment with men whose egos are dying is akin to those who prepare men for marriage. All men need to learn how to focus on their first interest when they enter marriage. Such a man seeks out the tempering of all egocentric interests to serve his spouse's needs. He yields these interests to healing so that the needs of the bride can be attended to with generous joy. Similarly, as self-interest diminishes in the ever-growing contemplation of God's beauty, the seminarian begins

---

15 "Therefore, if you have been raised with Christ, keep seeking the things that are above, where Christ is, seated at the right hand of God.... For you have died, and your life is hidden with Christ in God. When Christ, who is our life, is revealed, then you also will be revealed with Him in glory." Col 3:1, 3–4.

From Loneliness to Solitude to Communion • 73

to experience that his own need to receive love can be done with less ego obstruction ("I deserve this or that"; "I should have been affirmed for this or that"). He does not take or control or manipulate the reception of love; instead, over time, he becomes accustomed to taking up the posture of a beggar, opening his hands each morning to receive the good gifts of the Father. In this stance of humility, he gradually lets go of demanding specific outcomes from the Lord and begins simply to find himself in the peaceful presence of God's benign countenance. This presence begins to suffice as his primary locus of affirmation. And, so, being affirmed by God, being so loved himself, he can confidently turn toward the pain of others in pastoral charity.

Trust

To a large extent, seminary spiritual direction exists to open the seminarian's eyes to two truths. The first is that *interior living is foundational to self-possession.* But such possession happens because a turning within is also a turning toward a Divine Person. To be a man of interiority is not simply to claim oneself in isolation. Within us is Another, as Saint Augustine discovered when he exclaimed about God: "You were within while I was outside."[16] In isolation from the indwelling God,

---

16 St. Augustine, *Confessions*, trans. John K. Ryan (Image, 1960), Book 10.27.

74 · The Spiritual Formation of Seminarians

Saint Augustine cast himself upon a false and unsatis-
factory rest in the things of "this age" (Rom 12:2). Instead
of this false rest, we direct the seminarians to entrust
themselves to the mystery of Christ as He shares Himself
at the eucharistic liturgy. The cross is the content and
invitation of the liturgy; there, it is celebrated as love
and transmitted as life. "Come to me, all you who labor
and are burdened, and I will give you rest" (Mt 11:28).
The rest, however, is the consolation of being with
Christ on the cross—paradoxical rest indeed. In truth,
we discover our identity as men in communion with
this self-offering of Christ. Seeking to maintain this
communion with Him, we can cast ourselves upon Him
in worship. Only in worship and as worshippers is our
true human identity known.

The second truth is that *failing to turn toward God from
within leads to moral blindness*, to not seeing the needs of
others. Thus, the whole public thrust of priesthood is lost
as one's ability to see the poor is darkened, threatening
pastoral charity. Leaving others "unseen" is a common
moral malady suffered by contemporary Western males.
It is a common task for formators to assist seminarians
coming from this culture to adjust their moral eyesight
so they might "see" others with empathy. This moral
and emotional ophthalmology is a significant concern of
formators, and spiritual directors need to assist as well.
To notice one's fellows is as significant a spiritual goal as
is noticing one's own affective movement in relation to

From Loneliness to Solitude to Communion · 75

God in prayer. Father Christopher Seith describes well the emotional and social condition of Western adolescent and young adult males:

> Limitation, desire, thirst—all of this technology has removed from our day-to-day experience. The result of this is a neutered spirit that can no longer experience joy because it can no longer experience desire. The person, so affected, becomes enslaved in acedia's kingdom. The noonday devil places a sorrowful lens over his eyes and imprisons him in a lonely, profaned, and superficial world. Such has been the devastation wrought by our digital devices. Of course, the reality is that our limitedness has not been overcome but merely ignored. Our thirst for the Infinite does not go away; it is just buried beneath layers and layers of information which pose as an answer to our thirst. Our desire is still there but we are sickened by it, like someone with a hangover is sickened by the thought of food. "The Infinite" appears loathsome to us. We do not want more information; we want reality. But to keep ourselves safe from [intimacy] we have numbed ourselves to reality. How do we solve this dilemma? The only way out is to renounce that spirit and live by faith. The opposite of the person imprisoned by acedia, then, is ... the

76 • The Spiritual Formation of Seminarians

> person who has seen something. And this vision has given him life. It is the one who has turned his eyes towards Jesus and has let the Lord live His Life within him."[17]

To enter spiritual direction in a seminary is to choose no longer to tolerate the "sorrowful lens" placed over one's eyes. It is to seek optic therapy. Not only has one grown blind to noticing the presence of others, but often one has also willfully hidden oneself so as to not risk intimacy, involvement. He has been wooed into a life of escape. Slowly, the director leads the seminarian out of his "hiding places" (Gn 3:8–9) that have robbed his desires and blinded his capacity for contemplating what is beautiful. Now the seminarian is invited to communion with the living God. As the director teaches prayer to the seminarian and listens to the content of his already existing prayer, the director encourages the man into a deeper trust. Moving into the loving gaze of the Holy Trinity for the seminarian will be a progressive and developmental movement. While listening for those hints where divine love is already being received and returned in the seminarian's prayer, the director counsels him to remain at those portals so they grow wider, more easily entered.

---

17 Christopher J. Seith, *Rekindling Wonder: Touching Heaven in a Screen Saturated World* (En Route Books and Media, 2022), 127.

From Loneliness to Solitude to Communion · 77

Intimacy is secured by mutual self-revelation. The Holy Trinity has already revealed Himself in the life, death, and resurrection of the Second Person; now, the seminarian is invited to trust that such revelation was for his good by a God who only wills his good. "This is the will of God, your holiness" (1 Thes 4:3). The invitation is clear: it is the seminarian's turn now to reveal himself to God in prayer. This revelation will involve a purifying passage from any addictions to fantasy, immediate gratification, or false independence. Such purification is at the service of welcoming an unobstructed vulnerability to God's loving presence. It will be this presence, over time and through self-denial, that becomes internalized through the seminarian's contemplation. This contemplative receptivity is vital to secure not only in affective intimacy with God through faith, hope, and love, but because it communicates the vocation of celibacy to the man. As I noted in chapter two, a woman's bodily presence brings marriage to the man who is truly wounded by her beauty. So it is God's eucharistic presence that brings celibacy to the man called to share in Christ's own. Thus, in receiving the person (the woman in one case, God Incarnate in the other), one receives his vocation. This is why teaching men to pray who are attracted to celibacy is so vital: In the personal reality of God encountered in prayer, one receives his future, his vocation, his way to holiness. The director leads a man in formation to consider if the joy he wants for himself is the joy he sees in God, a joy in

78 · The Spiritual Formation of Seminarians

God with whom he is meant to unite, just as for a man called to marriage, it is a joy he sees in a woman, a joy in *the* woman with whom he is meant to unite. Here, prayer clarifies personal desire.

Ultimately, perhaps after some initial resistance, a vocation is always one's most desirous way of living in Christ. Our vocation is to carry us through our lives and ought never, itself, be a cross. If our vocation is merely a "cross" (something we choose but are not attracted to in love), we will be crushed when more suffering is encountered within the vocation itself. One's vocation is chosen in joy since it is the consolation that supports us as we hang upon the suffering given to us by life according to the Father's will. We share in the cross of Christ when we meet evil with love. We share in the joy of Christ when we choose to come and follow Him (Mt 4:19) as He calls us to our vocation.

Loneliness, Solitude, Celibacy

Within vocational conversations between a director and a seminarian, the theme of loneliness frequently arises. Loneliness is a part of the human condition and not simply a sign that something is personally wrong with an individual. Of course, some people bring on their own loneliness by remaining in behaviors or character traits that may push others away from them. Such moral or affective wounds must be dealt with in seminary formation; otherwise, such a man can never be

From Loneliness to Solitude to Communion · 79

"a bridge" to Christ in ministry, as I discussed in chapter one.[18] Loneliness can also befall a man through the evil executed by others, and hence, one can become a victim of loneliness through no fault of his own.

Universally, however, loneliness awakens human beings to our destiny as persons in communion with one another and God. We experience loneliness as pain, and rightly, we seek a remedy. Something in our being cries out that such isolation is not good for humans, not the way life was meant to be. The remedy for existential loneliness is our vocation maturely embraced and lived out. Spiritual direction can be an aid in drawing a man out of loneliness by leading him into the communion that is contemplative prayer. Loneliness is sometimes hard to identify in oneself both socially and spiritually as it is a source of shame ("Why don't others approve of me?") or guilt ("What did I do wrong to feel so isolated?"; "Why is my prayer so emotionally empty and dry?"). As a result, some men choose not to look at loneliness and the pain that accompanies it. Helping a seminarian first admit his loneliness is vital. Only when he can name the suffering of being alone (Gn 2:18) can he discern if his joy is to be found in woman as mediator of holiness (marriage) or found in the source of her beauty and joy, God Himself (celibacy). Discerning this joy, he can then over time move into a life of peaceful communion with God as a celibate.

18 *Ratio fundamentalis*, no. 63; see also *Pastores dabo vobis*, no. 43.

80 • The Spiritual Formation of Seminarians

If a man keeps associating being alone with a negative judgment, a sign of personal failure or rejection, he will be constrained from resting for long in solitude. In such a case, solitude is construed as loneliness. Loneliness is emotional pain, and such pain usually drives a man to seek activity, even frenetically, to soothe the pain. This activity can be as varied as self-initiated ministry, simple socializing, or engaging sporting past times. Such self-initiated busy-ness can be born when emotional pain is isolated within the self (the seminarian judging himself as rejected or broken or insufficient). Here, loneliness can lead to sin, to acts that artificially console the self. Instead, the director counsels the seminarian to relate his loneliness to God in prayer. Unrelated emotional pain breeds unconscious coping behavior.

Spiritual direction creates a different trajectory. It assists a man to move from loneliness to solitude to communion with God in prayer. Solitude differs from loneliness in that it is the anticipation of forthcoming communion, whereas loneliness is the pain of communion denied or withdrawn. To attain such communion, the seminarian must suffer a transition from feeling loneliness to welcoming the silence of solitude as the occasion for noticing a new depth of Divine Presence, not its absence. How does direction move a man from loneliness to communion through an embrace of solitude and silence?

First, the director needs to listen for the seminarian's experience of chaste celibacy. Does it seem obligatory, or imposed as an obedience, or does he experience it as the bent of his personality devoid of supernatural origin? Is the seminarian "learning" celibacy, embracing it more consciously as a gift given from God, as a sharing in Christ's own celibacy? Again, this "sharing" is not to be seen simply as moral emulation of Christ ("I am celibate because Christ was single"). Such emulation can become extrinsic to the man; it can feel like a weight of striving or "fixing" oneself to be more like Christ.

What the director is looking for is a growing awareness in the seminarian that celibacy is his way of staying with the Holy Trinity, a way that appears "easiest" for him to become a saint. The director will notice in this growing awareness if there is a true maturity in the man regarding his view of marriage or if he is simply choosing "bachelorhood." In the mature heterosexual male, foregoing marriage will always carry a sacrifice within it; but it is a sacrifice contextualized in the larger invitation he is receiving from God to a contemplative eroticism, a life of deep prayer and loving spousal surrender to both God and the needs of the Church as his first interest.[19] So, the director is, first and foremost, listening to hear if the seminarian is choosing celibacy from within a conscious experience of the supernatural, perhaps nascent but maturing.

---

19 For more on sacrifice and contemplative eroticism, see James Keating, "Sexual Integrity in the Formation of Seminarians," in *Sex and the Spiritual Life: Reclaiming Integrity, Wholeness, and Intimacy*, ed. Patricia Cooney Hathaway (Ave Maria Press, 2020), 153–67.

Second, the director attends to the pain of loneliness that the seminarian may be reporting. This pain will be mild in many seminarians but can be deep in a few. Is the loneliness part of a larger personality weakness ("I just can't seem to make and keep friends"; "I don't know what to do in prayer"; "I can't connect my interior life to God")? Does the seminarian need to be counseled by the seminary counselor to free up his affective life? The director may suggest this path if he hears a stubborn pattern of frustration in the man regarding his capacity to rest in the bonds of friendship or deeper prayer. One always comes to God with one's humanity intact, so if the seminarian is reporting challenges in human relationships, he is probably having challenges remaining in intimate prayer as well. This human condition is why the Church sees the need to have all four areas of formation be in communication with each other (with due regard for each area's level of confidentiality) for the sake of integrated growth in each seminarian.

Third, simultaneously with any needed counseling, the director progressively introduces the seminarian to periods of deeper and longer silence. Intentional silence is a true suffering today as seminarians emerge from popular culture and enter seminary oriented toward sound, or even noise, as their native land. Devoid of sound, the seminarian may enter prayer disoriented and anxious. It is necessary that the director be very exact in describing what happens in silence to help allay fears and prevent any premature ending of prayer due to

From Loneliness to Solitude to Communion · 83

emotional distress. Since the popular culture is saturated with noise, committing oneself to silent prayer is one of the most challenging spiritual disciplines in current Western culture.

The director, therefore, needs to introduce the seminarian to a motivation for prayer deeper than the one he has inhabited before coming to seminary. "Shallow prayer" will not carry a man from the culture of noise and immediate gratification through to solitude and into communion. Such shallow prayer leaves the seminarian "at risk" of abandoning prayer altogether or simply living a single life and mimicking vocational celibacy.[20] By faking celibacy, I mean a life of hiding in a routine or a structure of habitual busy-ness, one that eschews deep communion with the Holy Trinity.[21] The true celibate is a

---

20 "It would be wrong to think that ordinary Christians can be content with a shallow prayer that is unable to fill their whole life. Especially in the face of the many trials to which today's world subjects faith, they would be not only mediocre Christians but 'Christians at risk.' They would run the insidious risk of seeing their faith progressively undermined, and would perhaps end up succumbing to the allure of substitutes.... It is therefore essential that *education in prayer* should become ... a key-point of all pastoral planning." John Paul II, Apostolic Letter *Novo millenio ineunte* (January 6, 2001), no. 34.

21 I therefore don't mean only those who are pretending to live a life of celibacy while secretly engaging in romantic or sexual encounters. However, those who start out with the intention of "white-knuckling" a celibate lifestyle, rather than

84 • The Spiritual Formation of Seminarians

true contemplative: one who, ordered by the theological virtues, finds bodily satisfaction in the Spirit through the sacraments as this Holy Spirit calls forth from the seminarian a capacity for affective sharing in a reciprocity of love with God.[22] How does direction, then, move a man from loneliness to communion? Authentic celibacy is discerned; loneliness is engaged as real and related to God in prayer, and silence is embraced as God's presence, not His absence. As noted above, one way to describe

---

receiving it as a divine gift, are also prone to eventually violating their vows when the loneliness becomes too great to bear or the opportunity arises. As with the need for seminarians to become contemplative, the insistence on a divine foundation for celibacy is not a case of simply raising the bar for what is expected of priests to some lofty ideal; it is practically more likely to avoid disaster and scandal as well.

22 This life of "bodily satisfaction in the Spirit" is foreshadowed in the example of Saint Joseph. "'Joseph ... took his wife; but he knew her not, until she had borne a son' (Mt 1:24–25). These words indicate another kind of closeness in marriage. The deep spiritual closeness arising from marital union and the interpersonal contact between man and woman have their definitive origin in the Spirit, the Giver of Life (cf. Jn 6:63). Joseph, in obedience to the Spirit, *found in the Spirit the source of love, the conjugal love which he experienced as a man. And this love proved to be greater than this 'just man' could ever have expected within the limits of his human heart.*" Pope John Paul II, Apostolic Exhortation *Redemptoris custos* (August 15, 1989), no. 19, emphasis added.

From Loneliness to Solitude to Communion · 85

priestly spirituality is a way of eucharistic contemplative intimacy unto self-gift or pastoral charity.

The formation staff is aware that sometimes, a man might try to go forward in priestly formation sustained by the schedule of the institution. He seeks to be carried into priesthood by simply checking the boxes of attendance at the next event that demands his presence. The director and formation staff are trying to invite a more intentional presence from the seminarian: Do you want to be with God in this holy hour? Why do you show up at the last minute? Do you want to share your whole life with God as a celibate? Why do you reveal to him only your pious thoughts and activities? Encouraging men to share the fullness of their lives with God in prayer, warts and all, slowly reveals to them what true intimacy is and how satisfying it can be to be known and still loved. Here begin the seeds of an authentic contemplative life.

Many seminarians, however, carry a distorted image of themselves into prayer. "I am sorry I have this body, Lord; if only I were a spirit, you would love me, and I would love myself." Here, the seminarian does not yet understand the Incarnation and meaning of salvation. He cannot believe that his faults and sins do not turn God away in the same way they make the seminarian hate himself. He is almost insulted that God's love is unconditional, that in receiving God's forgiveness, he can no longer use his sins as a basis for self-hate, which he mistakes as humility or even repentance. The process of

86 · The Spiritual Formation of Seminarians

deepening one's presence to God in prayer requires both self-revelation and suffering the healing needed regarding these distortions to identity.

This takes a great deal of patience. Seminarians want to rush intimacy with God and sometimes get lost in a mode of fixing themselves morally. This fixing is attempted for the purpose of putting no obstructions between themselves and divine intimacy, but itfurthers the myth that God loves only "the perfect." In doing this, they tend to get lost in their own heads; they engage in an exhausting monologue of self-criticism and impatience with their own humanity. There are some seminarians that turn toward self-analysis, probing their motives for sin, trying to "figure out" why they are attracted to any one of the seven deadly sins. Thus they leave the presence of the Holy Trinity and turn away from the Divine Healer. They wander off alone into a desert of meditation on sin, which is never meditation's proper object.

In some cases, due to emotional trauma, perhaps, seminarians can develop their own moral code. They become their own legislators and follow a code born of promises or vows made as a result of the emotional trauma, perhaps far in excess of the commandments and precepts of the Church. "I will always call my mother on Tuesday," thinks one man, since this man's brother renounced the family and stopped all communication. "I will pay attention to other people's faults so I can help them," thinks another, since he is embarrassed to be associated with men in formation who reflect

From Loneliness to Solitude to Communion • 87

poorly his own self-image. The director must help the man see that his inner voice telling him to "do this" or "do that" may not be the voice of conscience formed in truth but formed by the aberration of truth due to emotional woundedness. Not every voice he hears issuing commands is God's. Slowly, the director moves the man to believe that moral healing comes from within the relational prayer he has with God, not from his own inner monologue about faults. Moral healing occurs in a divine relationship.

In contrast to this monologue, prayer involves "an act of interior detachment and of conversion, a self-surrender that disengages us from the things that drag us down and distort us, in order once again to open ourselves to God."[23] Faith-wise, seminarians can tend to forget a vital attribute of God: He is looking for us (Gn 3:9; Lk 15:19–20; Lk 14:23). God wants to be with us more than we want to attain moral goodness. When seminarians have a breakthrough (experience of affective love from God) or a breakdown (reach the limits of trying to "fix" or save themselves) in their prayer and emotional life, they can begin to believe this truth about God more earnestly. But such liberation from perfecting the self can take some time, and the director needs to revisit this debilitating habit on a regular basis, slowly having seminarians choose to look at the life, death, and resurrection of Christ more than their own progress in perfection.

---

23 Daniélou, *Prayer: The Mission of the Church*, 22.

88 · The Spiritual Formation of Seminarians

Another block to intimacy with God is a man's secret belief that his sins have offended God so much that God's love for him is at risk.[24] Begun in a concrete historical act (a sin, a lack of trust regarding his vocation, an act of failure, etc.), the seminarian keeps the fruit of this act—"God doesn't love me,"—a secret. This belief, hidden out of shame, appears only when the director gently probes around revelations regarding self-worth or lack of trust in God, or expressions of self-denigration, even those made in jest. This belief can also be exposed by the director listening "between the lines" when the seminarian reports disproportionate emotional responses to peers' teasing or judgments made against him ("Oh, Joe will never get this answer" or "Joe, I'm sure God talks to you all the time").

The seminarian may report he felt anger over being teased. Such teasing "shut down my emotions toward my brother seminarians" or the like. In asking why such

---

24 Or that his love for God is at risk, which is of course possible only in the case of mortal sin and not in failing to call his mother on Tuesdays. The director needs to point the scrupulous man back to the objective teachings of the Church regarding what constitutes grave matter and full consent, and to the confessional as the place of healing for even the most grievous offenses. Of course, as with all seminary staff, the director also should be alert to signs of catastrophic moral failings (unchastity, dishonesty, disobedience, etc.) that demonstrate a character unfit for ordination, without denying that God's love is faithful even to the unfaithful (2 Tim 2:13).

From Loneliness to Solitude to Communion • 89

comments bothered the seminarian, the director listens for unintentionally revealed facts about the seminarian's relationship with God or false understandings he holds regarding the identity of God. "I hate when I get angry at the guys; I know I can do better. God wants me to do better." Here, the man begins to peel back this insidious lie that lives in his depths: "I am a disappointment to God." It may take several sessions for this one to be named so honestly, but when the seminarian hears himself say that (or something similar) out loud, he can now name the wound. Inviting the seminarian to bring this lie before God in prayer can heal and restore vibrant intimacy to his prayer life. An emotional wound is healed when we no longer make conclusions out of its pain or act out of it behaviorally. We may always remember the incident (forms of abuse or trauma), but when we are healed, our actions no longer emanate from the site of the original incident; the power it possesses over the unconscious is depleted.

Ecstasy

So much of the early stages of seminarian prayer—be they at the discipleship or configuration stage of formation—are simply days of suffering God's presence unto intimacy. Most seminarians are at a point their spiritual lives where seminary is exploratory. They cannot simply enter formation assured that priesthood is their calling. There is so much healing needed around their capacity

90 • The Spiritual Formation of Seminarians

for affective intimacy, trust, and self-donation. God brings celibacy with Him to a man who has suffered a new capacity for contemplative prayer. It is necessary for spiritual directors to teach seminarians simply to go to prayer being desirous of His presence. Most seminarians want to be in prayer to "get answers." They go to holy hour each day hoping that one day, they will hear a locution telling them, "Go home and get married," or "You are my priest." The director invites the seminarian simply to rest in the presence of God. He is to delight in this presence the way he would delight in the presence of a romantic interest. "I am choosing to be with you." As a man regularly desires and chooses to be with a woman, she will carry within her own person a proposal for marriage or simply the invitation to friendship. The relationship itself carries and reveals the vocation to the one who is vulnerable, attentive, and realistic. The same is true for the celibate vocation.

The seminarian needs to be vulnerable in prayer until God moves from being simply an idea in his mind ("I believe") to a person he knows and loves. As prayer deepens, matures, the seminarian becomes aware that, often, he was not fully or really in the presence of God as his object of love. Instead, the seminarian was simply thinking about God as he remembered Him from literary or homiletic descriptions (or thinking about a hundred other things). God had not fully emerged as a person. Until this personalization of God is gifted to the man, any choice for celibacy may remain at the institutional

From Loneliness to Solitude to Communion • 91

or unexamined level. A fair number of seminarians are still trying to "find" God in a complete way, and they use props or reading or routines to anchor their prayer time. All this is well and good, even necessary. As time progresses over the years of formation, they will grow restless within these rituals; God is moving them a bit deeper into His presence, and the directors are guiding them to trust that He is in this restlessness.

In the early stages of formation, some men speak of being in the seminary "out of duty," knowing there is a shortage of priests. This approach imitates the motivation of those who might join the military or volunteer fire department knowing that the welfare of the city calls to them. But can a man become a celibate priest out of duty? It may be argued that yes, one can enter priesthood out of duty, with knowledge given through the theological virtues. If this may be true, the dutiful man still needs to understand a way to live priesthood that fulfills his needs for affective intimacy. The human love and regard of parishioners alone cannot carry this need. If this source is relied upon too much, the priest might even become a burden to his own people. Perhaps the celibate would meet these affective needs within friendship? But might this not reduce the call to celibacy to a form of bachelorhood? Deeper still, beyond friendship, is the need for consoling affective intimacy by way of the reciprocity of personal love; this is the erotic norm for human beings. This need is usually filled within the spousal relationship, but for the celibate cleric, it is

92 • The Spiritual Formation of Seminarians

fulfilled within contemplative prayer. Not to pursue such intimacy in prayer with the Most Holy Trinity is to court a life short of abundant living (Jn 10:10).

It is for the seminarian's own moral and spiritual good that formation probes deeply into his affective life. It serves neither his own nor the Church's good if his affective needs are ignored, minimized, or wrongly placed during formation and into priestly life. Communion with the Holy Trinity gives clerical celibacy its very reason to be. A man needs to be involved in a beauty (*kallos*) which summons self-donation. For most men, this beauty is the woman; for the sacerdotal celibate, it is the beauty of God as revealed in Christ's self-donative sacrifice for the sake of the Church, celebrated in the eucharistic liturgy, and internalized in personal prayer. "Intercourse" with beauty is not optional for a man. Such is his deepest interest as doing so renders him life-giving and not self-enclosed.[25] A non-praying priest may render dutiful service, but a praying priest will gift himself to others out of fulfilled desire in contemplative love of God. Affective maturity demands that one only serves, only gives, from a heart already full of being loved, from a disinterested heart. Without such erotic contemplative prayer, the Church

---

25 See Robert Louis Wilken, "Blessed Passion of Love: The Affections, the Church Fathers, and the Christian Life," in *The Spirit, the Affections, and the Christian Tradition*, ed. Dale M. Coulter and Amos Yong (University of Notre Dame Press, 2016), esp. 35–36.

From Loneliness to Solitude to Communion · 93

gets bureaucrats and not lovers, that is, spiritual sterility and not fecundity. The erotic movement of the heart and body toward its object of attraction is not self-serving or fastened upon bodily pleasure. The erotic signals the human being's desire to transcend the self, and it leads to an agape—a self-donation"—that does not end in burnout or cynicism.

"True, *eros* tends to rise 'in ecstasy' towards the Divine, to lead us beyond ourselves; yet for this very reason it calls for a path of ascent, renunciation, purification and healing."[26] This fuller sense of the erotic places the celibate in a life of self-emptying so as to be filled with the Divine love that is attracting him. God moves a man out of self-interest into a new fascination with God's own beauty. This God is close and reveals His heart generously to those who suffer His coming into their lives. Some diocesan priests may argue that such a vision of celibate priesthood is excessive in its mysticism. To them, to be a bureaucrat or benevolent servant seems sufficient motivation for serving the needs of the Church, especially when such service is rendered as the gifts of administration and governance. Even noting that exercising the gift of administration and abiding with parishioners out of a benevolent heart are valid and vital parts of the priestly life, the spiritual director has the responsibility to explore a seminarian's capacity to enter "unceasing

---

26 Pope Benedict XVI, Encyclical Letter *Deus caritas est* (December 25, 2005), no. 5; see also, Cooper, *Holy Eros*, 18–23.

94 • The Spiritual Formation of Seminarians

intimacy" with God. Indeed, only in this way will he be prepared as a priest to see the presence of Christ in the "distressing disguise" of his flock.

The seminarian needs to explore with his director and God whether Divine Beauty alone is enough for his body to rest within. The "bureaucrats" (those who Pope Francis calls the careerists) among the seminarians may resist this intimacy or ignore this invitation, but the director has the responsibility to offer "the more." "The main task of those responsible for the running of seminaries is the formation of the students in interior silence.... A seminary must realize that it is preparing future 'spiritual directors.'"[27] Here, we see that the Church Herself calls for a priesthood that goes deeper than loyal servant or benevolent administrator, since such a functionary would be ill-equipped to be a spiritual advisor.[28] Pope Benedict

---

27 Sacred Congregation for Catholic Education, "Circular Letter Concerning Some of the More Urgent Aspects of Spiritual Formation in Seminaries" [Jan. 6, 1980], *Origins* 9, no. 38 (March 6, 1980): 610–19, available at https://www.usccb.org/ beliefs-and-teachings/vocations/priesthood/priestly-formation/ church-documents-for-priestly-formation.

28 The consciousness of the Church has expanded regarding this portion of the priestly vocation and now, rightly, invites more specific and deeper training for clerics beyond seminary before they begin directing souls. However, the formation of the diocesan priest, when it honors interiority, inner healing, and tutoring in contemplative prayer and discernment, is certainly sufficient training for him to accompany parishioners in their spiritual needs.

XVI pointed in the direction of a more contemplative celibate priest as well:

> Do not become utterly absorbed in activism. There would be so much to do that one could be working on it constantly.... Not becoming totally absorbed in activism means ... remaining with God.... One should not feel obligated to work ceaselessly; [a cleric has] to leave things to others so as to maintain his inner view of the whole, his interior recollection, from which the view of what is essential can proceed.[29]

What a powerful summation of the origin of ministry in the diocesan priest: "From which the view of what is essential can proceed." Discerning what is "essential" in ministry flows from an interior communion with God and not simply from skill sets and organizational sensibilities. Such aptitude alone is not sufficient for either the personal happiness of the celibate priest or the spiritual needs of the parishioners he serves.

The director is not looking only for those especially inclined to a contemplative life, the "super prayers" as it were, but rather to ensure that every priest has

---

29 Pope Benedict XVI, *Light of the World: The Pope, the Church, and the Signs of the Times* (Ignatius Press, 2010), 71–72; see also James Keating, *Configured to Christ: On Spiritual Direction and Clergy Formation* (Emmaus Road Publishing, 2021), chapter 9.

the simple but essential level of intimacy necessary to keep a relationship with the Holy Trinity alive. This is analogous to marriage—not every relationship is a storybook romance, full of bliss, but there must be a baseline of intimacy to keep it from falling into division and even ruin. The institution of the priesthood, like the institution of marriage, has become fragile amidst the impermanence of modern culture—if merely social incentives and roles were ever enough to sustain a lifetime commitment in prior generations, they no longer suffice. Without some level of intimacy with God, the priest is quite likely to burn out from their "much serving" and leave the ministry in search of some other fulfillment. Or, worse, to join in the duplicity and corruption of those who abuse their ecclesiastical office and even the people of God for the sake of personal gratification or glorification. By contrast, those who root themselves in Christ will be prepared for the disappointments and frustrations of working for a hierarchal Church made up of fallible (and in some cases, vicious) human beings, as well as for the lack of encouragement or even scorn that may come at them from the wider secular culture and even from the faithful themselves. One can only appreciate the Church as "the mystical Body of Christ" (*Lumen Gentium* 8) if one is, at least to some extent, a mystic.

Four

Formed in Word and Sacrament

The mysticism required of the Catholic priest is a "sacramental mysticism," indeed, a eucharistic mysticism.[1] To facilitate his maintaining an "inner view of the whole," the priestly aspirant is immersed in the eucharistic mysteries through all the stages of formation.[2] "Participation in the daily celebration of Eucharist ... should permeate the life of the seminarian."[3] Each day in his worship, the seminarian deepens his participation in the life of the Holy Trinity. "One thing is clear: the daily Eucharist has to be the heart of any formation for the priesthood. The chapel must constitute the center of the seminary, and staying close to the Eucharist has to

---

1 Benedict XVI, *Deus caritas est*, nos. 13 and 14.

2 Benedict XVI, *Light of the World*, 72.

3 *Ratio fundamentalis*, no. 104.

98 · The Spiritual Formation of Seminarians

be continued and deepened by personal prayer in the presence of the Lord."[4]

Even though the seminarian sits among many peers at worship, he still comes to God as a distinct person. Due to this personal element in corporate worship, a spiritual director is charged to attend to the fruit of eucharistic worship with each seminarian. The director is invited to listen for evidence that the seminarian is integrating personal prayer and his discernment of celibacy into his worship at the Mass. Even in and among other believers, the seminarian must surrender himself into the mystery of Christ's own surrender to the Father. This surrender to the Father is at the core of the Christ's own sonship. It was this surrender to and trust of the Heavenly Father that enabled divine life to issue forth from Christ's ministry of healing, teaching, and raising dead hearts and bodies to life. Christ wishes to share this sonship with seminarians.

The man's experience of human sonship colors his reception of adopted, divine sonship. Integrating personal prayer into Christ's own self-offering at Mass to the Father may be slowed for any number of aspirants if their earthly fathers were emotionally absent from

---

4 Joseph Cardinal Ratzinger, "Some Perspectives on Priestly Formation Today," in *The Catholic Priest as Moral Teacher and Guide: Proceedings of Symposium Held at St. Charles Borromeo Seminary, Overbrook, Pennsylvania, January 17–20, 1990* (Ignatius Press, 1990), 18.

Formed in Word and Sacrament • 99

them. The seminarian's turn toward the Father in Christ's own sonship is a healing prayer that may facilitate any needed forgiveness between son and dad. Such a healing is called for in both human and spiritual formation. When a seminarian experiences his dad poorly communicating sonship to him, it leaves a wound where there should be a blessing. In such cases, the son-seminarian can turn to the perfect Father in heaven to love him. But in most cases, no one has ever taught him how to do so in Christ. Left on his own, the son-seminarian may have stalled emotionally and failed to mature in his sonship. Thus, he is left ill-prepared to become a spiritual father himself as priest. In having such a wounded relationship with his own dad, he may inadvertently mistrust Our Father in heaven as well.

In this case, the director will notice resentment in the seminarian's own heart toward God: "Why did God abandon me to such an absent earthly dad?" If such a seminarian reveals this father wound to his formators, the resources of the seminary can begin to facilitate the seminarian's future forgiveness of his earthly dad. This forgiveness can awaken a new consciousness within the seminarian that God the Father's actions were reaching him all along despite his dad's emotional absence. Contextualizing this healing within the man's participation in the Eucharist is vital, as such worship occurs daily, and the seminarian can serenely offer his pain in and through Christ's own offering of His Body to the Father. Such a configuration to Christ in faith will secure proper emotional safety for the seminarian as the Spirit searches his heart to ease the barriers that exist between himself and paternal love. It is unfortunate for a man, and unfair to the Church, if one becomes a priest amid unsettled anger or resentment against his own father.

This is one example of emotional and moral healing in the context of the Eucharist, but the liturgy is a font of healing for the seminarian in a universal way. Not only does worship constitute a man's correct orientation toward God the Father in Christ but, progressively and developmentally, this worship bears to him the fruits of freedom from sin and the healing of his affection for sin through the years of formation. Obviously, becoming a free man emotionally and morally is not the first purpose of eucharistic worship. But within the context of its end as a communal act of thanksgiving and praise to the Father in communion with the Body and Blood of Christ, it is a source of conversion and purification.[5]

Inviting the seminarian to enter worship with the hope of being renewed in his spiritual and moral life highlights the personal encounter with Christ the liturgy provides him each day. By hoping in this encounter, the seminarian learns to love going to Mass, not simply as a duty of justice toward God but as a living communion with the Trinity. Such daily worship has immeasurable personal consequences to his current spiritual life and future ministry as a priest. "Our own contribution to the

---

5 *Catechism of the Catholic Church*, nos. 1392, 1394, 1436.

liturgy consists only in accepting grace, in not wasting the treasure, in not extinguishing the lamp once lit.... In fact, however, in this contribution, there is room for the entire moral commitment of the Christian."[6] To accept grace is to enter the Eucharist at its white-hot center. This center is a participation in the real presence of Christ, His sacrifice and resurrection, and a holy communion with the Trinity that saves from sin and precisely because this is daily liturgical worship secures one's relationship with God. For a seminarian to become vulnerable to the life and love of God as unveiled and offered at the Eucharist is to have him lay the foundation for priesthood in his own body. Further, and as a fruit of his participation in the Eucharist, the seminarian is invited by his director to notice God calling, consoling, or challenging him throughout the day. This noticing assists in deepening intimacy between the aspirant and God. Finally, as a eucharistic fruit, a seminarian is to simply notice God's presence releasing joy within the heart. Being with Goodness itself in the ways noted above cannot fail to release joy. Does the seminarian place himself in the Divine Presence in these ways? Are these dispositions known and ordered toward hosting God in the seminarian's daily routine? Directors cannot assume such features dwell intrinsically in men of the Western culture in the twenty-first century.

---

6 Raniero Cantalamessa, *The Mystery of Easter* (Liturgical Press, 1993), 60.

102 · The Spiritual Formation of Seminarians

As the men in formation choose to participate more deeply in formation, they must also choose to participate more deeply in the Eucharist. To do so is apt for their vocation as it is the place where they offer their bodies to the One who is offering His true body both to the Father and to them. The priesthood they seek as their vocation is conditioned upon this mutual gift of surrender. Encompassed by the Eucharist, the formation that engages the candidate seeks to impart the ways of pastoral charity, service, as built upon faith, hope, and love. This participatory formation yields a mature, faith-inspired, and healed masculine identity. Such a man gifts himself to an ecclesial life of executing charity through the power of that sacrament, the Eucharist, that contains the very presence of the One who is Charity. This man of service, in other words, is open to receive a level of service (deacon) that becomes sacrifice (priest), a share in Christ's own.[7] The seminarian is being formed in this service-become-sacrifice every day at Mass, joining his own will to that of the One who offered such a gift to the Father in the first place. Such a process of relational self-offering within the Eucharist reaches its crescendo when a deacon lies upon the cathedral floor and rises to priesthood. The director invites the seminarian to reveal in their sessions the levels of participation God is drawing him into within this sacramental energy.

---

7 John Paul II, *Pastores dabo vobis*, no. 21.

Daily Worship

Experientially, the daily Mass is both a gift and task for the seminarian. Its regular availability is a gift too deep for words, a privilege rarely known in the Church universally. And yet, this same availability can also be experienced as "routine" for the seminarian—or worse, at times, a burden. It becomes a burden not because it is ill appreciated, but because it has a weight coextensive with the "daily schedule." The spiritual director needs to notice if daily Eucharist is becoming "routine" or emotionally burdensome and explore this aspect of seminary formation with the men he guides.

Seminarians need to see the daily Eucharist as true "food for the journey." Food is that which keeps us alive, nourishing our blood that circulates through the whole body. Spiritually, the Eucharist is the daily food that circulates through a man's faith, hope, and love, thus keeping alive his relationship with the Holy Trinity. Even on a natural level, eating together is an opportunity for bonding and the building of relationships, although in contemporary Western culture, we have often reduced meals to an individualized consumption of calories. Consuming food in a context of abundance can become routine, so only the deepening of the virtue of gratitude prevents such from descending into entitlement. Seminarians may also fall into ingratitude towards daily worship, discovering that their attention toward it is diffused and their presence distracted by the

104 · The Spiritual Formation of Seminarians

weighty aspects of daily life, exams, pastoral assignments, personal emotional struggles, and so on.

With such life experiences weighing on their time and emotions, seminarians might understandably imagine regular worship as a speedbump inhibiting progress in achieving daily duties. Ironically, placing worship in such a "useless" category defines both its glory and our culture's descent into pragmatism as the overriding norm. Of course, deadlines press against the leisure of worship, but the director must also help the seminarian face the reality that other concerns can dislodge what ought to be his first interest in life: worship of the Holy Trinity. This kind of experience is akin to a spousal situation where concerns in one's profession are making it difficult to give attention to one's spouse or children. If such a situation lingers, it can weaken the communion within that marriage or family.

It is also vital to point out that it is the relationship with God that is central for the seminarian's life's meaning. The relationship remains even after the emotions are healed or the test is passed, or the pastoral situation resolves itself. Will the seminarian find a way to guard this relationship when these concerns press upon him? Alternately, will the seminarian learn how to simply deepen his gratitude to God even when the routine carries no deadlines or pressing problems to solve? In struggling to be attentive to the presence of Christ in the eucharistic liturgy, is the seminarian indicating a lingering need for novelty, distraction, or new

Formed in Word and Sacrament • 105

experiences? How will this need serve him in the future as the mundane duties of parish life fail to entertain or serve up variety? We can remind and invite the seminarian to remember that the Eucharist is not about him but about what God is doing. "The mystery that is Christ is the center of Christian life, and it is this mystery and nothing else, that the church renews in the liturgy so that we might be drawn into it."[8] Assisting a seminarian to sort out his authentic attitude toward daily worship is most vital within his formation as a "man of discernment." Is he attracted to the Eucharist as a real encounter with the Holy Trinity? Can he become vulnerable to the truth of the Eucharist each day even if he experiences little affective movements during worship?

Forming the men to attend to even the slightest affective movement carrying grace is a helpful goal of seminary spiritual direction. It is rare that worship leaves a man void of any affective movement, but such movements can be so slight that a man alienated from his own interiority might miss them. Again, one ought not to seek an emotional experience in worship as a daily goal. We form the seminarian to simply worship, not to place his own agenda as the centerpiece. He is to surrender and be drawn up into the Paschal Mystery. However, due to the generosity of God, there is real

---

8 Robert P. Imbelli, *Rekindling the Christic Imagination: Theological Meditations for the New Evangelization* (Liturgical Press, 2014), 50.

cause to assist seminarians to "look again" when they report that worship has grown barren, and they resist surrendering to it due to an absence of affectivity. They may be looking for an "experience" when God is simply beholding them in love. The most real things in life can often be the least emotionally stimulating. One need only think of a constant presence of a spouse, a presence so continual that one can lose sight of its giftedness. But if that presence is lost, one's consciousness is overwhelmed with grief, aflame with the realization that the spouse's presence was the most vital part of one's life. The person of the spouse was not constantly "stimulating" or "entertaining," a fount of "experiences." No, presence is not continually charged with emotional energy, but there are few things in life that are more real and, therefore, more worth attending to no matter the "payoff" at the level of ego stimulation.

But again, rare is the Mass that will not yield some affective movement. God knows we need help adhering more deeply to the mystery that is His Divine Presence. Directors teach seminarians how to notice even the "still small voice" (1 Kgs 19:12). Worship is about gratitude directed to His presence and self-surrender by the power of the Holy Spirit, offered to God the Father in and through the saving mystery of Christ. Worship is the central act of a man's life. Due to this, the need for seminarians to be present at daily Eucharist is self-evident. Even still, the influential formation of social media has trained the seminarian to expect quick responses to his

Formed in Word and Sacrament • 107

needs and thoughts. The Eucharist, although certainly a sensory experience, may be judged by tech-inundated seminarians to be a rather passive one.[9] It is vital that spiritual directors explore with seminarians what it means for them to be "really present" in every situation. Being formed into restlessness by the media of instant gratification presents obstacles inhibiting men to transition into the less stimulating arenas such as worship, study, and listening to the needs of others. Ministry is for the affectively mature. It calls for a man to be present as gift more so than as recipient.

Obviously, seminarians must be formed to receive love from God as their anthropological foundation if they are to be radically present in ministry. And that reception of love is best done in prayer and worship. Pope Benedict XVI, addressing the bishops of Brazil in April 2010, said, "The main, fundamental attitude of the Christian faithful who take part in the liturgical celebration is not action but listening, opening themselves, receiving."[10] Such receptivity is not passive but active. A man must want

---

9 See Dicastery for Communication, *Towards a Full Presence: A Pastoral Reflection on Engagement with Social Media* (May 28, 2023), no. 60 and following pages. A good resource for all things digital is seminary psychologist Dr. Christina Lynch's *Born Digital: Psychological Perspectives of Human and Spiritual Formation in the Digital Age* (Published by the author, 2022).

10 Quoted in Office for the Liturgical Celebrations of the Supreme Pontiff, "To Enter into the Christian Mystery Through the Rites and Prayers" (September 7, 2010).

108 · The Spiritual Formation of Seminarians

to be in the presence of God, want to open his heart to be affected by grace, to develop a habit of asking the Lord for grace and healing, to consciously unite his own trials and struggles with the sacrifice of the altar. Even though worship is receptive, it is not akin to being passively entertained or distracted by the next event on the seminary schedule. In worship, the seminarian is called to be receptively engaged by the Paschal Mystery reaching him, inviting him to participate. Without spiritual directors engendering this commitment on the part of seminarians to remain present receiving and giving love amid salvation being offered at the Mass, and in their relational prayer, the Church risks sending celibate men into ministry who may meet their affective needs through inappropriate means. As mature mediators of grace, clerics are formed to rightly order both their need for love and self-donation toward God, so they may direct their parishioners' desires ultimately toward this same end.

Developing the capacity to notice affective movements from God is built upon one embracing interior silence, a silence that makes evident when interior communion with God has been severed. Such evidence is found when one's emotions signal distress or leave the soul anxious or angry or adrift in boredom. As the director attunes a man to such interior phenomenon, he is training the seminarian to remain present first to himself, so that he might detect and admit that "I am lonely" and second, to detect God, "Come to me" (Mt 11:28). Such formation

Formed in Word and Sacrament · 109

in silent listening is progressive and developmental. Eventually, as one abides within a silent, listening heart, the goal of inner awareness is attained. This awareness is not an end in itself but simply the content of what is shared in the self-revelatory dialogue that is prayer. Inner awareness is facilitated by the gentle coaxing of the director to have the seminarian pay attention to his thoughts, feelings, and desires. In this silent awareness, he can better notice God moving toward his own heart.

Silence in the Eucharist

As noted above and earlier in the book, silence is a vital component within the Catholic spiritual life. Presently, I want to meditate upon the silence within the eucharistic liturgy. There are still many priests who shy away from silence within the Mass. They do so for many reasons, both practical and liturgical. I would like to argue that the seminary priestly staff should be role models in how to incorporate silence into the liturgy. Without silence, there can be no profound adoration within the Mass. Adoration is not simply to be reserved for the "holy hour" as an extension of the mystery celebrated; adoration is intrinsic to the Mass and, thus, so is silence.[11]

"Receiving the Eucharist means adoring him whom we receive. Only in this way do we become one with him....

---

11 Lawrence Feingold, *The Eucharist: Mystery of Presence, Sacrifice, and Communion* (Emmaus Academic, 2018), 597.

110 · The Spiritual Formation of Seminarians

'Only in adoration can a profound and genuine reception mature.'[12] Within the Mass is time for adoration, briefly at the elevation of the species and lengthier after reception of Holy Communion. It is this time after Holy Communion that I consider vital for helping the men mature in appropriating chaste celibacy. What should happen during this time of silence, and how can directors assist the seminarian to be fully present within it? First, directors should reflect upon these truths about the Eucharist:

> Therefore when we eat and drink [the Eucharist], our body is nourished by immortality, for it participates in the immortal flesh of Jesus.... In the Eucharist we can become sons in the Son, fed by the bread that comes from the mouth of God.... Because it contains the entire life of Christ, the Eucharist also takes up all of history, which is recapitulated by him, starting with the history of Israel.[13]

---

12 Pope Benedict XVI, Post-Synodal Apostolic Exhortation *Sacramentum caritatis* (February 22, 2007), no. 66. See also no. 50: "The precious time of thanksgiving after communion should not be neglected: besides the singing of an appropriate hymn, it can also be most helpful to remain recollected in silence. " See also, James Keating, "Silence as Participation in Worship," *The Priest* (June 15, 2022), https://thepriest.com/2022/06/15/silence-as-participation-in-worship/.

13 José Granados, *Introduction to Sacramental Theology: Signs of Christ in the Flesh* (The Catholic University of America Press, 2021), 86–87.

Such a profound daily event, encapsulating these potent realities—"the entire life of Christ," "all of history," "immortality"—deserves a seminarian's adoration and praise right when it is being offered. To facilitate such reception, directors ought to promote the provision within Mass for a prudential length of silence after Holy Communion. Seminarians need this lengthier silence as it is this very mystery received that is inviting them into celibacy. "Be still before the Lord; wait for him" (Ps 37:7).

Secondly, directors should spend some time with seminarians imparting ways that promote an active receptivity to their participation in daily Mass. Remote preparation occurs in the seminarian's ever deeper grasp of the gift that is *lectio divina*, which I will discuss in further detail in the next chapter. Besides the man's attachment to Scripture (*lectio*) as encounter with God in prayer, the director encourages the seminarian to prepare for Mass as the true highlight of each day. Objectively, such is the case doctrinally; now, it must become so personally for his celibate heart as well.[14] One helpful way to assist the man toward active receptivity at Mass is to discuss the eucharistic fast with him.

David Fagerberg noted that asceticism is the process of "finding Christ attractive: it is erotic training."[15] To deny oneself food before participating in the sacramental

---

14 *Catechism of the Catholic Church*, no. 1324.

15 David W. Fagerberg, *On Liturgical Asceticism* (The Catholic University of America Press, 2013), 159.

112 • The Spiritual Formation of Seminarians

expression of the life, death, and resurrection of Christ is an attempt over many years to replace one longing, food, for another, participation in the circulation of Divine Love. Directors would do well to regularly converse with seminarians about what attachments are keeping them from longing for a life of ceaseless prayer as the foundation for pastoral charity (1 Thes 5:16). It is fitting to inquire about this longing in spiritual direction because what is at stake is the man's own happiness as celibate. Ultimately, the only sound reason to find celibacy attractive is because a person finds prayer attractive, that is, one's deepest erotic longing is to remain in communion with the Trinity. Service in the Church does not require celibacy. It can be accomplished as an act of charity or competence by married persons and single chaste persons. To be an affectively and spiritually fulfilled celibate, he must want prayer, even hunger for it. This is why the silence in the Mass at a seminary is vital. It reaches up and around and within the seminarian, carrying a vital question: Are you at peace in my presence? Or do you seek a mediated rest in Me through a woman? What is your deepest longing? Where will it find fulfillment?

By fasting, the seminarian is better prepared to enter a deeper silence at the Eucharist. In fasting, the seminarian refrains from bodily nourishment to call forth a spiritual hunger satisfied in his sharing sacramentally in the life of Christ. What he feeds on at Mass is the very reality that wants to satisfy both his body and soul in the celibate life: the life-giving self-donation of the Bridegroom crucified

Formed in Word and Sacrament · 113

and risen. In order to be celibate and not simply a bachelor or "single" in the service of availability, a seminarian needs to be possessed by the mystery of the Bridegroom and the Bride, the relationship between Christ and the Church. That is, he needs to both receive the love of the Holy Trinity in his body day after day at the Eucharist and then share this same love ministerially with Christ's Body, with those who seek healing through Divine Love. Those who maintain a celibate witness in the Church, especially diocesan priests, cultivate the art of eucharistic and spousal accompaniment by carving out in their hearts a space of love for Church members founded upon their love for God.

> John Paul II says in *Vita Consecrata* §59 that this "space in the heart" is a Eucharistic space, and so the mark of a "spousal" existence, which has as its emblem a single-hearted devotion to Christ, and therefore a love for all whom Christ loves. This is the "sacramental 'mysticism'" to which Benedict XVI refers in *Deus Caritas Est* (§14).[16]

Devotion to Christ irrevocably gives rise to devotion to what or whom He loves, His Bride, the Church.

---

16 John Cavadini, "Celibacy in the Church and the Priesthood," *Church Life Journal* (June 2, 2023), https://churchlifejournal.nd.edu/articles/celibacy-in-the-church-and-the-priesthood/.

114 · The Spiritual Formation of Seminarians

Directors cannot neglect this reciprocal dynamic of receptivity giving rise to generativity. Such generativity—that is, ministry—hinges upon a seminarian's deep vulnerability to being loved by participating in the Paschal Mystery. As a celibate minister, the cleric truly needs to receive the Sacred Body "given for you" to know and be known by Love. Otherwise, where will he receive the love a spouse needs to receive? Where will his erotic hunger be fulfilled? Without the hunger for God finding its satiation in the regular reception of Holy Communion, the seminarian remains at risk of simply being "single." What is this risk and who might suffer because of its possibility? We return to John Paul II who identified the spiritual risk that awaits those who enter only shallow prayer[17]: such men inevitably find substitutes for God. Indeed, substitutes for God loom large for the seminarian if his prayer remains only at the level of ritual and not at the level of erotic fulfillment. Just as the lay man must learn to find affective rest in a mature and prayer-guided relationship with his wife, the seminarian needs guidance in learning how his *desire to be known* is fulfilled by God in contemplative prayer. Such contemplation is executed both privately and within the public liturgy. Utilizing the time given within the liturgy for silence, and some further silence after the Mass has concluded, comes to anchor the longer times of silent love in a regular holy hour, or within *lectio divina*. To hunger for God, to seek

---

17 See John Paul II, *Novo millenio ineunte*, no. 34.

Him in silence is to finally experience Him as a personal reality and not simply as an "idea" to intellectually understand or a cause to serve.

God as Person Who Heals

Relating to and identifying God as an idea is common in seminarians in the early stages of formation. They are surprised, and maybe even ashamed, when they realize they have not been relating to God in prayer but only thinking about God. But such a habit is not uncommon, and the director should assure them that there is no need for shame, only growth. To relate to God as a person and move from simply thinking about Him can only be achieved through the long, slow, and suffered experience of relational prayer. Moving a man from God-as-Idea to God-as-Person, to whom one can give one's body throughout life, is a dramatic move indeed. A director can only assess that this move has begun when the man begins to "like" being with God in silence. By "like," I do not mean the man simply likes being alone, likes the calm, likes quiet environments. By like, I mean he prays because he desires a presence beyond his own. Now, he desires a person, a relationship.

He is even willing to deny other "hungers" to have this substantive longing fulfilled by prayer—hence, fasting from food and drink is preparation for communion with God. Fasting is an opportunity to reject substitute gods (superficial consolations) and fast from them, eventually

116 · The Spiritual Formation of Seminarians

losing interest in them altogether. This includes fasting from certain forms of technology. When he does so, he senses that the hypnotic effect of media engaged him, feeding only his habit of pleasure seeking and escape. Saint Augustine seems to have emphasized fasting as both a way to separate ourselves from self-involvement and a way to "enrich the mind ... unto spiritual delight in wisdom."[18] We grow heavy and burdened when earthly goods are readily available. Formators are invited to assist the seminarian to renounce such heaviness and grow lighter and nimbler in mind and heart. This lighter heart is born when it fastens upon the things of God. To enter the eucharistic fast, and other kinds of fasting throughout the seminary formation year, is to deepen both spiritual and human formation at their source. St. Thomas observes:

> No other sacrament has greater healing power; through it sins are purged away, virtues are increased, and the soul is enriched with an abundance of every spiritual gift.... Yet, in the end, no one can fully express the sweetness of this sacrament, in which spiritual delight is tasted at its very source, and in which we renew the memory of that surpassing love for us which Christ revealed in his passion.[19]

18 Allan D. Fitzgerald, ed., *Augustine Through the Ages: An Encyclopedia* (Eerdmans, 1999), 355.

19 Thomas Aquinas, *Opusculum* 57, On the Feast of Corpus Christi, lect. 1–4, emphasis added.

Formed in Word and Sacrament · 117

Such fasting further excites a true hunger to accomplish the end of the seminarian's formative journey: Christic configuration. "But he said to them, 'I have food to eat of which you do not know.' So, the disciples said to one another, 'Could someone have brought him something to eat?' Jesus said to them, 'My food is to do the will of the one who sent me and to finish his work'" (Jn 4:32–34). The Eucharist is the formative therapy promoting such configuration, one that provides an antiseptic to the wounds caused by sin and simultaneously alters any previous repulsion toward divine obedience. Such obedience becomes desired spiritual nourishment.

Over time, the Eucharist can heal a seminarian's tendency to self-isolate from God. This ill-chosen isolation reflects a man's effort to heal his own wounds. When such healing is "accomplished," he thinks, he will then be ready to present himself to God as worthy. Directors will be keen to listen for this tendency within a man to fix himself; they can then patiently lead him in another direction. One direction would be to ponder this truth: "It was relationships that wounded you (family of origin wounds, premature romantic involvements, rejection by friends, and so on), and it will be *remaining in the One relationship* with the Trinity that will heal you." There is no healing found in isolated rumination or in exerting a tactical moral willing. A seminarian leaving aside his relationship with God to concentrate upon personal problem-solving is done to demonic delight. Even when legitimate venues are chosen

118 · The Spiritual Formation of Seminarians

to process personal wounds, such as formation advising or psychological counseling, a man should envelop these in prayer or bring their contents to prayer after the session has been completed. Coming to see themselves as embedded in relatedness can facilitate emotional and spiritual healing in seminarians, a healing born of deep communion with God in worship and prayer.

A great deal of seminary spiritual direction pivots around reminding men to stay in communion, that is, to stay in communion through everything they are experiencing and choosing. Now, no one can always remain in conscious communion with God; that occurs only after death. But to yield one's interior life to the presence of God throughout the day is the only way one's life will open to heaven in the end. Seeing their lives constituted by a secure relationship with God teaches seminarians that intimacy with God is the norm for those choosing Holy Orders. Within such intimacy, and as the ground for such, a man can share his wounds with the Most Holy Trinity and not be ashamed in the sharing. Some seminarians think that God only "likes" them when they are "perfect," and that such perfection is the goal. Shame shrinks prayer. Shame, feeling like a hypocrite (especially regarding sexual sins) can weigh heavily upon a seminarian and collude with satanic temptation to make the man's prayer tepid and superficial. "I should be better by now, especially in light of prayer experiences I have had."

As opposed to true repentance, shame leads the seminarian to lean on his own strength and reasoning

Formed in Word and Sacrament · 119

to "manage" his sins. The director is to remind the seminarian that "perfect love casts out all fear" (1 Jn 4:18) and correct him that such perfect love is not established in the seminarian's will alone. No, it is Jesus's perfect love that is casting out fear in the seminarian, *not* the seminarian willing to love perfectly. "Sin management" is a popular coping mechanism with seminarians who try to achieve peace of mind in light of their own incongruency in faith development. This management takes the form of withholding the truth from God about their weaknesses until they set up a "strategy" for new behavior. It is this new behavior that will please God. The director needs to listen deeply to the seminarian until that seminarian realizes that what God wants from the seminarian is not perfection but communication. God is inviting the man to reveal to Him all of the seminarian's thoughts, feelings, and desires. It may take time for the man to believe that God truly wants all of what resides in his heart to become the content of prayer ... good thoughts, feelings, and desires, but also evil ones. This process of self-revelation anchors a heart in God's unconditional love.

When the interior of a man is revealed to God, that heart is taken possession of by Christ. A man's affection for his sins begins to heal. God takes possession of the wound from which sin and erroneous thinking are born and forbids the man to have a claim on it anymore. It is His to heal, and it is the seminarian's to forget. We invite the seminarian to ask the Spirit to move him away from doing any of his thinking out of his wounds, such as resentment, personal rejection, lust, perfection striving, people pleasing, and so on. The seminarian transitions to a freedom that positions his thinking to be the fruit of his relationship with God. This established relationship and the intimate sharing at its heart are now a furnace for the healing of emotional and moral wounds. Such healing will not happen if the seminarian loses patience and moves back to the same place that bred the wounds: isolation. Communion becomes the new locus of his interior world. Such communion is secured by the seminarian when he notices he is electing to go "it alone" and resists such a move. Directors encourage a man to no longer let his thoughts drag him to isolation, thus courting desolation. In such a life, when communion with the Eucharist is deeply internalized, a man is liberated from inhabiting isolation and instead becomes a native of the liturgy. Within the eucharistic liturgy lies the unveiled Word of God and the veiled Body of Christ, crucified and risen, under the appearance of bread and wine. Before these, the seminarian is bid to "unveil" his own heart in prayer.

Lectio

Such unveiled prayer flows from and into the mystery of the Word of God proclaimed and the shared Body and Blood of the Incarnate Word. "To be formed in the spirit of the Gospel, the interior man needs to take special and faithful care of the interior spiritual life ... nourished by

Formed in Word and Sacrament • 121

… meditation on the inspired Word."[20] This prayerful meditation upon the Word, internalized and longed for, renders the seminarian capable of discernment. The *Ratio fundamentalis* describes:

> Priestly formation is a journey of transformation that renews the heart and mind of the person, so that he can "*discern what is the will of God, what is good and pleasing and perfect*" (cf. Rom 12:2). Indeed, the gradual inner growth along the journey of formation should principally be aimed at making the future priest a "man of discernment", able to read the reality of human life in the light of the Spirit.[21]

To be in the Word of God is essential for the preacher-priest, and such prayerful attention to the Scriptures is not a rival to his duties toward academic study. Study is introductory and preparatory for a lifetime of prayerful *lectio* as priest. "Study is concerned with scientific certitude; lectio wishes to nourish a spiritual experience. Study takes place on the objective and detached level of investigation; lectio takes place in the contemplative atmosphere of prayer."[22] *Lectio* is a personal encounter

---

20 *Ratio fundamentalis*, no. 42.

21 *Ratio fundamentalis*, no. 43.

22 Mariano Magrassi, OSB, *Praying the Bible: An Introduction to Lectio Divina* (Liturgical Press, 1998), 73.

with God by way of prayerfully engaging the text. "Lectio is ... an affective reading ... because it is an encounter with a person. ... Sacred reading is relational, a listening to the Risen Lord ... speaking through ... sacred words."[23] The *Ratio* notes that academic study helps the seminarian to "listen profoundly to the word of God"[24] as well as to become a man of discernment. Both the spiritual approach to Scripture in *lectio* and the scientific approach to Scripture in the classroom form the one man who ministers pastoral charity. Such charity flows out of a heart resting in contemplative receptivity to the Word of God, which is an encounter with a living Person. Both *lectio* and study conspire to form a priest who leads parishioners confidently toward God. Priestly formation is a mode of living within which intellectual formation is integral but does not overwhelm other formative dimensions.[25]

Noting this integral role of academic formation, directors will utilize *lectio divina* at every stage of formation

---

23 Laurence Kriegshauser, OSB, "Western Monastic Tradition of Lectio Divina and Seminary Formation," in *Piercing the Clouds: Lectio Divina and Preparation for Ministry*, ed. Kevin Zilverburg and Scott Carl (Saint Paul Seminary Press, 2021), 22–24. This book is a must-read for seminary spiritual directors. I also recommend: James Keating, ed. *Lectio Divina: Assimilating the Holy Word in Seminary Formation* (Institute for Priestly Formation, 2023).

24 *Ratio fundamentalis*, no. 117.

25 *Ratio fundamentalis*, no. 118.

Formed in Word and Sacrament · 123

to sensitize their capacity to encounter God in the text. Possessing such sensitivity, the seminarian is in no danger of reducing the Bible to a textbook. The director encourages the man to set no limit as to how he may be drawn into the life of Christ. Intimacy in prayerful reading of Scripture augurs well for ordaining a man whose interior life is sound. It is one built upon both docile theological reading and prayerful receptivity to Christ dwelling in the Scriptures.

Lectio divina as an encounter in faith with the living God can be transformative of a man's intellect and affect. It can be inspiring and healing. The power of forming a man in *lectio* is so convincing that Benedict XVI once predicted that *lectio*, when done consistently and vulnerably, will bring the Church into "a new spiritual springtime."[26] Future priests should certainly be schooled in the habit that would usher such a springtime into parish life. What approach might a director take to teaching *lectio*?

Lectio divina is a reading until one is ushered into the Divine Presence; it is a listening until one hears

---

26 Pope Benedict XVI, "Address to the Participants in the International Congress Organized to Commemorate the 40th Anniversary of the Dogmatic Constitution on Divine Revelation *Dei Verbum*" (September 16, 2005); one can read of the other formational effects of *lectio* in Raymond Studzinski, OSB, *Reading to Live: The Evolving Practice of Lectio Divina* (Liturgical Press, 2009), 192–219.

something. Such reading and listening is done under the sign of the cross. Such a discipline is not simply meditation, because its aim is to be gifted with time in the presence of God. The director invites the seminarian to remain in silence for a few minutes, allowing the distractions of the present moment in and out of his mind and heart under the power of the Holy Spirit. The man is to notice and then let go of the clutter filling his interior. At a moment of stillness, he is to begin *lectio* under the sign of the cross, further chasing away demonic interference. As his heart is readied by the silence and protected by the cross, he is to begin reading, listening to the text. If possible, it is best to read the text out loud, deliberately lingering over the ideas, images, and affections that the text is eliciting. When one or more of these elicitations carries the weight of an encounter, he is to pause and welcome God into his heart at a deeper, more intentional, and active level of engagement. With God, he allows the content of the arresting text to become a dialogue between himself and the indwelling Spirit. The seminarian is to host this presence until his heart is full of the fruit received through faith, hope, and love. The nature of this fruit is worth discussing in detail, and so I will do so in the next chapter.

Five

An Ascetical Devotion

As noted above, "The seminarian needs to be vulnerable in prayer until God moves from being simply an idea ("I believe") to a person he knows and loves." As I began to discuss at the end of the last chapter, *Lectio divina* is a determined way to move a man from relating to God as only an idea to encountering Him as a person. This occurs in the interaction between a seminarian's faith-filled approach to Scripture and God's movement to the man through the text of His Word. The images and words, envisioned and read, stir the seminarian's intellect and affect and so become internalized. This internalization of content carries the truth to the seminarian, a truth that we know is the person of Christ (Jn 14:6).[1]

---

1 "'What is truth?' (Jn 18:37, 38). Pilate cannot understand that 'the' Truth is standing in front of him, he cannot see in Jesus the face of the truth that is the face of God. And yet Jesus

126 • The Spiritual Formation of Seminarians

Such internalizing—resulting from one's beholding of the Word prayerfully—gives the Spirit an opportunity to gift the seminarian with knowledge of Christ as living. In this gift, Christ as only an idea is ushered out of his imagination. In encouraging the seminarians to let the presence of Christ affect them, his formators hope they will learn to relax in His company. The goal would be to have seminarians desire *lectio* as an opportunity to be with the person of Christ.

As men's prayer deepens, and they learns to enjoy the company of the Holy Trinity, they also develop their capacity to notice lesser motives for prayer. One such lesser motive is attending to *lectio* and contemplative prayer as performance. Approaching prayer as performance can have its roots in seminarians' younger lives when parental attention was gained by their performance in sports, academic work, music, theater, or other avocations. Prayer can be the occasion for this unconscious childhood habit operating as a motive. Here, the seminarian would be disposed toward God in the same way he was as a boy toward his parents. Prayer would act analogously to his searching the grandstands to see if mom or dad were present to see him play school

---

is exactly this: the Truth that, in the fullness of time, 'became flesh' (cf. Jn 1:1, 14), and came to dwell among us so that we might know it. The truth is not grasped as a thing, the truth is encountered. It is not a possession; it is an encounter with a Person." Pope Francis, *L'Osservatore Romano* (May 22, 2013): 3.

sports or perform in the school play. The still-developing heart hoped to gain approval, affirmation, or a parental blessing solely by means of his actions. Unknowingly, seminarians may approach prayer in the same way they may have garnered parental approval. This search for God's approval ("See; I am praying") adds undue stress to prayer. When prayer is entered as performance, it is not desired for itself. Instead, it becomes a time to continue the quest for authority's approval, either God's or the formation staff's. Once such an unconscious motive is exposed and accepted, the director can lead the seminarian toward a more mature grasp of what prayer is and why it is so essential in the celibate life.

The nature of *lectio* is very helpful here in healing any mixed motives for entering prayer. *Lectio* draws the seminarian into a real communion with the very person of Christ through the contemplation of His historical actions and words. These components of Christ's life continue in the present through the grace of the Holy Spirit and affect the seminarian's commitment to prayer. Christ is still teaching, still healing, still inviting to conversion through the ministry of the Church. Christ's presence is most concentrated in the sacraments, but the seminarian's experience of Him becomes more and more personal, more real, more engaging in Himself through *lectio*. Due to this practice, the seminarian can let go of any immature reason to pray and yield to the real presence of God in faith as his ever-deepening foundation for prayer. It is a vital component in the history of

128 · The Spiritual Formation of Seminarians

lectio that this kind of prayer stir a man's affect.[2] Such movement secures an adherence to Christ, one that becomes a source of desire and imagination. In *lectio*, the seminarian learns that Christ is still teaching, healing, and converting him. Prayerful reading is personal.

In introducing relational prayer to seminarians, we often emphasize its self-revelatory aspect for the seminarian. This is vital since many men do not yet know how to notice their desires, thoughts, and feelings; and, so, they need to be made aware of them. In becoming aware, the man can then share his interior life with the Holy Trinity in prayer. This tutoring in interiority, however, may inadvertently cause the seminarian's prayer to become self-focused—encouraging the very tendency, ironically, that prayer is trying to heal. For prayer to become a settled communion within the man, he needs to become awakened and possess an interest in God's own life. This opening up to possess an interest in God is attained in *lectio* when the man becomes interested in Christ's own interior movements. For example, when the man is pondering the crucifixion scene, he might ask Christ in prayer, "What were *your* thoughts, feelings, and desires as you saw the ones you love give in to the temptation to torture and crucify you?" Or, at the healing of the lepers, the seminarian might wonder, "What were

---

2 As noted in chapter 4 above: Kriegshauser, "Western Monastic Tradition of *Lectio Divina* and Seminary Formation," 22–23.

An Ascetical Devotion · 129

your thoughts, feelings, and desires, Christ, when only one leper returned in gratitude?" Prayer, the seminarian discovers, is not simply him pouring his heart out to Christ in response to Christ's self-revelation in the Paschal Mystery. Prayer is also interest in the real person of Christ and His interior experience. We are to encourage the seminarian to ask the Holy Spirit to unleash such interest in Christ's own heart if the seminarian finds himself stuck in a kind of self-exploration of feelings instead of real prayer.

Even though affect is an essential part of prayer, it can appear absent at intermittent periods of a man's prayer life. The absence of affect in prayer, or in motivation to pray, can be a burden to many. In this case, the director reminds the man that often in a lifetime of prayer, we are carried more deeply into communion with God by faith and not through gratifying feelings. Faith is essential if prayer is to deepen; faith is the very substance of prayer. But faith is not a merely intellectual virtue that captures a man to live cerebrally, to live in one's head. In a life of prayer, the journey of faith involves our full humanity; and, so, common testimony reports that faith-filled prayer involves the activation of affectivity. The man is not wrong to think that the presence of good feelings or consoling feelings in prayer is normal. This is attested to, not contradicted, by the burden in contemplative prayer known as the dark night. The dark night would not be so weighty in its effects upon a person's faith life if the absence of God positively moving affections were not a norm in prayer.

130 • The Spiritual Formation of Seminarians

Faithfulness in relation to prayer, sometimes referred to by seminarians as fulfilling their "duty," is functional but not optimal, especially for lifelong celibate living. A mature male is called to have a lively and engaged affective life. He is not expected to simply live for duty alone, any more than it is normal for a married man to relate to his spouse through duty alone. The understanding of faith solely as duty can be encouraged by a limited definition of faith that identifies it as a life congruent with doctrinal truth. Such an approach, as I noted, is functional but not optimal for a celibate. Rather, he is called to have God as his first interest, an interest so real, so lively that he notices a desire to forego marriage and chooses to do so. As a celibate priest, he chooses to remain with this first interest until death. We are called as directors to explore any lack of affect in relation to prayer with the man who reports such. Prayer by its very nature is relational. In such cases of low affect, spiritual directors and seminary counselors work in harmony within their own spheres of confidentiality, actively inviting such a man to reveal his suffering within the appropriate forum. Obviously, such low affect can simply be God purifying a man's reliance upon habits of immediate gratification, or it may be a sign of something more sustained, such as depression.[3]

---

3 "I have treated many depressed individuals who were sustained during their periods of darkness by their faith in God the father's love—although they could not always feel or

An Ascetical Devotion · 131

Here is an ancillary reason formators ought to encourage faith-sharing groups among its seminarians. During the testimonies shared and received within such groups, seminarians may become aware that their prayer is devoid of affect or notice that the fruit of others' prayer appears different than their own. Such listening within these public groups may prompt a man with low affect in prayer to consult with his director or counselor. "When I listen to my brother seminarians, their prayer is full of affective responses whereas I am beginning to notice that my prayer encompasses meditation and thinking but little affect." In revealing this, a seminarian may discover, for example, that such was the communication method he was raised on within his own home or among early companions, hence he did not know other possible experiences of prayer or intimate communication were available to him.

---

sense this love affectively, they knew in faith that God would not abandon them to ... despair." Aaron Kheriaty and John Cihak, *The Catholic Guide to Depression: How the Saints, the Sacraments, and Psychiatry Can Help You Break Its Grip and Find Happiness Again* (Sophia Institute Press, 2012), 207. Faith can sustain one through trial, but relational prayer is more akin to "life and life to the full" than simply sustenance. Hence, having seminarians consult psychological experts when prayer involves low or no affective movement over time is prudent, just as having seminarians with excessive affectivity attend to the discipline of reason found within theology assists in their integration as men.

132 • The Spiritual Formation of Seminarians

The goal of prayer and *lectio* is not simply to "feel something," but it is to encounter in faith the God that wills a man become fully alive, fully integrated in reason, will, and affect. Can a man become a priest out of duty with little desire welling up in him to be with God in prayer? Yes, of course one can. But as I noted, this is not optimal but functional. The goal of formation is to invite a man to an integrated life, life to the full (Jn 10:10). One is called by the seminary formation team to welcome truth but to welcome it within an ambit of love. A seminarian may proceed through early formation "living in his head," but if he cooperates with formation, the truth sets him free to love and notice and even feel the Divine Presence. This is not to say that a man should seek out celibacy simply to feel God loving him in prayer; as in marriage, feelings are a means of connection in relationship, not an end in themselves. Alternately, a seminarian may proceed through early formation stages eschewing intellectual formation as a necessary evil so he can become a pastoral presence to those who suffer; but if he cooperates with formation, his strong affections will become founded upon the truth, securing an even deeper presence to those who need salvation preached to them. Here, the formation team is dedicated to expanding this man's understanding of what vocation to pastoral charity as priest really encompasses.

When a seminarian approaches *lectio* with little history of knowing Divine Love, his vulnerability to God through his reading can be the occasion to birth

An Ascetical Devotion • 133

affective movements ignited by the Truth found there, the truth that is a Person. Approaching *lectio* in faith, the man undergoes purification, a healing that may release him from any addiction to immediate gratification. *Lectio* can also work as a healing agent, occupying the divide between affect and intellect. As *lectio* teaches the men to welcome interior silence, to become skilled at noticing affective movements, it also aids their becoming adept at welcoming the grace of even a passing visit from God. The smallest movement from God toward them is not missed; they become content and not tempted to demand major spiritual experiences from God in prayer. Resting in His presence becomes a new goal and even a new habit.

Indeed, the prayerful reading of the Word is the most effective way for a seminarian to internalize the truths revealed there. Through such internalization, the future priest stores up substance for the Holy Spirit to work with, to draw from, in preparation for preaching, pastoral counseling, and confession. Without the habit of *lectio*, bolstered by prayerful theological study, a cleric is condemned to rely on his own opinions, perhaps gleaned from common opinion or, worse, partisan thought and ideologies. *Lectio*, and by extension, the prayerful study of theology, purifies and matures a seminarian's thinking and frees his mind from being captive to "this age" (Rom 12:1–2).

As the Word settles into the heart of the seminarian, so does the desire to relate his life to the One being revealed and encountered there. The Word becomes a

134 · The Spiritual Formation of Seminarians

touchstone of presence analogous to a visit to the Blessed Sacrament for silent prayer. For the celibate, seeking the presence of God is the very reason for his living such a sacrificial life. The seminarian's ever deepening engagement with the Scripture in prayer secures his mind and will to be in communion with God. As Benedict XVI noted, "Knowing God [study, academic competency] is not enough. For a true encounter with him one must also love him. Knowledge must become love."[4] As we encourage the seminarians not to give up on their habit of *lectio*, we remind them that the Word works deep within the unconscious, and the Spirit carries grace and insight to those depths to nourish the heart by this Living Word.[5] Benedict has reminded seminarians that philosophical ideas will come and go according to university fashions, but they must "study always with the Lord, before the Lord, and for Him."[6] Such immersion in the Word as anchor for the mind and heart establishes within the seminarian a touchstone of sanity. In this immersion, the man imitates the example of the Blessed Mother and the saints. As Angela Franks notes,

> The Magnificat sings Mary's gratitude and praise to the God who has lifted up Daughter

---

4 Pope Emeritus Benedict XVI, *Called to Holiness: On Love, Vocation, and Formation*, ed. Pietro Rossotti (The Catholic University of America Press, 2017), 177.

5 Benedict XVI, *Called to Holiness*, 200.

6 Benedict XVI, *Called to Holiness*, 236.

Zion, reweaving biblical imagery and quotation into its new historical setting at the moment of the Visitation. Likewise, the *Confessions* use God's words in Scripture to form the words of Augustine's confession of his lowliness and of God's creative mercy in his life. Their words to confess themselves and God must come from the personal divine Word, as expressed in the Scriptures and derived from his creative speech, which is a "[participation] in the Word" through whom all things were made.[7]

Being in the Word is to receive an identity that is given, sustained, and deepened relationally, never in isolation. So many vocational "crises" within a seminarian occur as he pulls out of this communion with the Word, thus isolating himself in susceptibility to follow the lie that he can "manage" on his own (cf. Gn 2:18).

The more the seminarian studies doctrine, theology, and Scripture in relationship to the Divine Presence, the freer he is from the enslavement to intellectual fashion. He prepares, therefore, to preach the word in season and out of season. Here, the Word of God is working on a man's imagination. It will be the imagination that sparks many an idea in the vocational and spiritual realm. And, so, the imagination must be born of an

---

7 Angela Franks, "Identity and the Trinitarian Imago," page 13 of typewritten manuscript.

136 · The Spiritual Formation of Seminarians

immersion in the life, death, and resurrection of Christ. Satan utilizes the imagination that is adrift, unmoored from the Paschal Mystery, to tempt and suggest modes of action or thinking. If followed by the will, these demonic suggestions can only lead a man to his "own place" once again (Acts 1:25). Set adrift from the Paschal Mystery, the imagination may itself be the occasion for confusion or simply self-involvement. By contrast, one can trust an imagination when it has been formed by the Paschal Mystery. As such, it can be used by the Spirit during *lectio* to deepen intimacy with God. We see the vital connection between worshipping the Father at the offering of the Paschal Mystery, the Mass, so that this holy event enters a person as his life's orientation. When life achieves this orientation, approaching Scripture in prayer can be done without concern. This orientation will see to it that going into the soul will not leave a man vulnerable to the "enemy."[8] As the imagination is filled with the Paschal Mystery, there is little concern that a man will find himself bereft of the Spirit's help while within his own soul. Of course, the director attends to such a man as another sure guide to interiority.

To instill *lectio* within seminarians as a spiritual habit does not happen quickly. This means that directors need to "check in" regularly to see that the seminarians are

---

8 Timothy Gallagher, OMV, *The Discernment of Spirits: An Ignatian Guide for Everyday Living* (The Crossroad Publishing Company, 2005), 32ff.

praying the Scriptures and maturing in their attentiveness to the Divine Presence that comes to them through the Word. It is good to ask them to give concrete testimony about how their commitment to *lectio* is growing within them. "The challenge [in seminary] is that the students are both learning about Scripture for the first time and seeking to read it prayerfully. It takes work to get the students to move from the head to the heart in their reading, to read slowly and carefully enough, and to apply it to themselves."[9] As with other disciplines, *lectio* can seem to some men "a cause not for joy but for pain" at first, but the more experienced seminarians can testify to the newer ones that "it brings the peaceful fruit of righteousness" to those who stick with it (Heb 12:11).

The Rosary

Related to *lectio* and more familiar to some of the men is the devotional practice of praying the rosary. This venerable practice is encouraged by the United States bishops in the 6th edition of the *Program for Priestly Formation*, particularly for its affective power and its effectiveness in a man's assimilating the mysteries of Christ.[10]

---

9 Peter S. Williamson, "Preparing Seminarians for the Ministry of the Word in Light of *Verbum Domini*," in *Verbum Domini and the Complementarity of Exegesis and Theology*, ed. Father Scott Carl (Eerdmans, 2015), 90.

10 *Program of Priestly Formation*, 6th ed., no. 229.

138 • The Spiritual Formation of Seminarians

"The Rosary, 'a compendium of the Gospel,' is especially recommended as a means of contemplating Christ in 'the School of Mary.'"[11] However, I have found that many men in seminary at first do not use the rosary as a means for contemplating the mysteries of Christ and, in fact, have trouble coordinating their meditation upon the mystery (the resurrection, for example), during the repetition of the Hail Mary prayer. Some use the prayer more as a method to "stay close" to the Blessed Mother in her intercessory power, especially regarding their desire for perfect chastity. This is, of course, something to encourage, but directors must also remind the seminarian that Mary is leading them into configuration to Christ and His own chastity by means of an intellectual and affective engagement with the mysteries of Christ's life and especially the Paschal Mystery. They should ask Mary to empower them into living Christ's own chastity and then turn their attention to the Lord Himself. I have found that an extensive catechesis on and practice of *lectio* helps the men enter the mystery of the rosary more easily. The events of Christ's life become internalized within their hearts, thus giving the Spirit much to work with when they meditate upon the mysteries with the Blessed Mother.

An exhaustive catechesis on the practice of *lectio* is best done in a theological class where the intellect can be energized in the face of the Christological mysteries. I would recommend that such a class occur within the

---

11 *Program of Priestly Formation*, 6th ed., no. 256.

An Ascetical Devotion · 139

seminary curriculum during the propaedeutic or discipleship stage. If the seminary also has a college program, it might be introduced there as well. Spiritual direction sessions, however, can bolster the truths learned in these classes through conversation and assess how their assimilation in the man's heart is progressing. Every director should routinely ask this question to directees: How did you experience God in class today, and how did your prayer become influenced by its grounding in the study of theology? Such conversations afford the seminarian time to internalize the mysteries of Christ's life and afford the Spirit rich fruit from which to draw as the men pray the rosary in a Christocentric way. Praying is the practice of uniting oneself to the One who is Love. The rosary is such a prayer through its process of leading the seminarian through the mysteries of Christ's own life.

The Examen

Approaching the Scriptures as an encounter with a living Divine Person and seeking out that encounter daily can deepen the capacity within a seminarian to welcome the interior movements of the Holy Spirit throughout daily events. Now the seminarian is learning not only self-awareness, but awareness of God's action within himself. The maturing of this capacity is crucial as one proceeds from discipleship to configuration stages and beyond. Such maturation can best be assisted through a seminarian's commitment to a daily examen of consciousness. The contemporary master of this prayer, which has its roots in Saint Ignatius of Loyola, is the late Jesuit Father George Aschenbrenner.[12] For Aschenbrenner, the examen is "an experience in faith of growing sensitivity to the unique, intimately special ways that God's Spirit has of approaching and calling us." It has as its prime concern "the way God is affecting and moving us ... deep in our own affective consciousness."[13] The examen is, in short, the habit of listening to God approach us and draw us to Himself throughout the day and then prayerfully noticing how we did or did not welcome Him during those times. Primarily, it is a commitment at some point in a seminarian's day to grow silent, turn within, and notice where he welcomed God during the day and allowed himself to be drawn into God's love, or where he might have resisted God's movement toward himself and chose to remain alone.

In teaching seminarians the examen, I first encourage them to understand that these are subtle divine movements toward them within their hearts. One must grow in interior silence to even notice many of the movements of God. However, once a man masters this kind of interior listening, when the time comes to practice the examen each day, his heart will be

---

12 George Aschenbrenner, SJ, *Quickening the Fire in Our Midst: The Challenge of Diocesan Priestly Spirituality* (Loyola Press, 2002), see especially 166–79.

13 Aschenbrenner, 167.

An Ascetical Devotion · 141

overflowing with knowledge of God's love for him. It is crucial that a priest be able to give testimony to his own experience of faith that God is alive and communicates with those who learn to listen. If a seminarian fails to master this kind of intimate communication with God, he will have fewer resources from which to draw as he encourages future parishioners to remain with God during the daily swirl of lay activities.

The examen can be an excellent way for a seminarian's faith to deepen and remain lively. Many times, when a seminarian comes for an appointment, I simply ask him to give testimony about how God loved him for the past two weeks. It is a privilege and a joy, and edifying to my own faith, to hear the stories of God's interaction with the men. As they mature in the examen, the men relate that they have difficulty not thinking about how God comes to love them in the daily events of seminary life. "God is too generous to me," they will say. Of course, this fullness is a result of the of men learning how to listen to God using their own affect and voice. Most of this communication is not dramatic; it is, in fact, ordinary. It is, in other words, God communicating Himself through the common stuff of human intimacy. In receiving such, the seminarian deepens his adherence to the Beloved. Maintaining such intimacy is *the* crucial goal of all prayer if the seminarian desires a commitment to interiority. As seminarians grow in the habit of the examen, as they listen all day for God (and not simply during scheduled prayer time), they come to delight in the particular and

142 • The Spiritual Formation of Seminarians

simple ways God deepens His presence to them: "As I walked by the chapel today, I heard Him say, 'Come and rest with me for a minute.'" "In class, I spaced out for a bit and heard God invite me to simply praise Him for second or two, and then He gently led me back to the lecture." "I noticed God was prompting me to go across the hallway to my fellow seminarian and seek his forgiveness for something I had said earlier," and so on.

For these men, God is living, communicating, and attractive. God is real! As we invite them to go deeper into *lectio* and practice the examen, the life, death, and resurrection of Christ becomes their imagination's touchstone. The Paschal Mystery begins to drift through their minds and hearts, regularly resulting in an imagination that is easily reached by the Spirit from within. The mind becomes saturated with God through *lectio* and the examen. Such prayer habits invite the Spirit to use the man's own thoughts and desires throughout the day as platforms for deepening communion between them. In this way, grounded by his regular participation in the Eucharist, a man begins to see the possibility of living a fulfilled celibate life. Such a life is not lonely. Such a life is not solitary. Such a life engages a personal reality, intimate and fulfilling. Seminarians "learn" celibacy, and assisting them in this knowledge is their growing consciousness of the presence of God. Engaging the Divine Presence moving within their hearts and minds is also crucial for their vocational discernment. Without the reality of this dynamic relationship between

An Ascetical Devotion · 143

themselves and God, their discernment might be reduced to an abstraction, a discussion of personal preferences and meeting external milestones. It might be embraced out of dutiful motivations rather than be a response to a personal call, a life of being "with him" (Mk 3:14).

Asceticism

The call to the priesthood is a call to take up one's cross and follow Christ, so it is no surprise that some seminarians are eager to embrace self-denial as a goal of formation. Nevertheless, directors must guide each man thoroughly in discerning what asceticism is and what it might mean to the seminarian. It is well known that unhealed emotional wounds and self-loathing over spiritual and moral failure can be a motivation when seeking to enact a practice of self-denial. These motives must be exposed and healed so that the man can freely enter a healthy and mature way of starving self-centeredness. Such self-denial and self-emptying is always enacted while a man remains open to Divine Love from the cross of Christ. The Church wants no regimen of self-denial that flows from any source other than a response to being so loved from the cross of Christ. We know that emotional insecurity and self-hate can be harbored deep within the hearts of those men who have yet to experience unconditional love. Events can trigger within a man the habit of responding to such out of insecurity or self-hate. Such insecurity can be healed only when unconditional love—the love of God

144 · The Spiritual Formation of Seminarians

from the cross—can reach those wounds in the heart born of rejection, fear, or self-loathing.

True asceticism can never be built upon unhealed wounds. Nevertheless, an attraction to asceticism is not in itself unhealthy, because "there is no holiness without renunciation."[14] What is renounced is not the deeper self as held in being by Trinitarian love but those more superficial aspects of life that gather around the self and threaten it with disintegration, with isolation from Trinitarian love. These realities must be renounced; they must be severed from the self as stumbling blocks to true worship. The call from the heart for an ascetical life is a call from the Spirit to put no obstacle between that heart and the voice of God.[15] The ascetical life into which directors want to invite seminarians is a life of becoming capable of worshipping the true God. True asceticism is a progressive renunciation of idolatry. As the men enter the battle of the spiritual life, the director attunes their inner ears to any voices that may call them away from the deepest liturgical participation, even the disordered attraction to natural goods like food or praise. The seminarian is to renounce those voices, enter the struggle of spiritual maturation and through grace refuse dalliance with temptation. The seminarian is encouraged to stand anew as a man who worships the real Word, the one Voice worth obeying. Asceticism forms

---

14 *Catechism of the Catholic Church*, no. 2015.

15 Fagerberg, *The Liturgical Cosmos*, 41.

men who listen and men who long. It also forms men who refuse to waste time responding to superficiality, self-involvement, and escapist pleasure. The material of the ascetical life is made up of that which is discerned by the director and seminarian in dialogue. The adventure into true worship cannot be spoiled by the possibility that a brittle foundation of emotional woundedness is its starting point.

Teaching Seminarians How to Listen

"St. Gregory posits the union of action with contemplation as the absolute ideal."[16] Discernment is the capacity to distinguish affective attraction to different goods. Which of a man's thoughts, feelings, and desires originate in his communion with God, and which ones spring from his capacity to isolate from God, allowing unhealed wounds or demonic sources to influence him? If seminary is about producing men of discernment, then that also means forming men who act out of relational prayer.[17] In other words, spiritual directors assist seminarians to become men who act in response to the beauty of the life, death, and resurrection of Christ and their love of it in prayer. As the future priest's life

---

16 Grazia Mangano Ragazzi, *Obeying the Truth: Discretion in the Spiritual Writings of Saint Catherine of Siena* (Oxford University Press, 2014), 118.

17 *Ratio fundamentalis*, no. 43.

146 · The Spiritual Formation of Seminarians

progresses, we want him to know that he does not have to act out of loneliness, isolation, or demonic captivity. By contemplating the Word, he becomes capable of discerning his inner thoughts, "taking captive" and rejecting those that isolate and come from pain or temptation (cf. 2 Cor 10:5) and embracing those that further divine communion.

Some seminarians reduce the act of listening to silent meditation or reading, but the director aims to teach that the mind cannot concentrate as long and as fully as can the heart and will. One listens with one's body, one's whole self. Affective and relational prayer applies "to all those movements of the will toward God ... it does not indicate any intensity of feeling or emotion.... It is a personal audience or a loving conversation with God, it is capable of as many variations as there are persons."[18] As the director tutors the seminarian in how to listen to God with his full being, he turns the man very gently toward "the profane human senses, making possible the act of faith, become spiritual."[19] In faith, we pass from seeing and hearing, from witness and testimony into a preparation for ecstasy and communion with the Holy Trinity. The spiritual sense of listening is a function of faith, not

---

18 Eugene Boylan, *Difficulties in Mental Prayer* (Christian Classics, 2010), 31–32.

19 Mark J. McInroy, "Karl Rahner and Hans Urs von Balthasar," in *The Spiritual Senses: Perceiving God in Western Christianity*, ed. Paul Gavrilyuk and Sarah Coakley (Cambridge University Press, 2013), 272.

An Ascetical Devotion · 147

sounds. What echoes in the ear of the heart is the mystery that indwells it. Such listening is preparation for ecstasy, not in the sense of continual pleasure, but in the sense of "going out of oneself" in pastoral charity. God wishes to draw a man out of himself in double ecstasy, toward both the heaven of the Holy Trinity and toward God's first interest on earth: those who suffer. For only the one who listens to God in faith and prayer can sustain a lifetime of ministry listening to and offered for the pain in the flesh and souls of parishioners. As the seminarian becomes more and more a man of the Liturgy of the Word, desiring *lectio* and resting in his daily examen (which bears the substance of his relationship to God in faith), he becomes more and more a man who apprehends the voice of God internally. He becomes a discerning priest.

Such personal intimacy and internalization can be further matured by a deepened and sustained instruction on how one is to spend time in adoration of the Blessed Sacrament. In this silent intimacy of the celebration of the Eucharist extended in time, a man can integrate the sacrificial self-gift of Christ that he receives at the Mass with an ever-deepening experience of *lectio* amidst his growing competency to recognize God's voice throughout an ordinary day. Directors encourage the men to commit to this devotion so as to make themselves available to be divinely loved. As I noted above regarding all prayer, such adoration has only one expectation: to present oneself lovingly to the loving Divine Presence and enter into it. Personal prayer, *lectio*, the Eucharist, the examen

148 · The Spiritual Formation of Seminarians

all conspire to gift a man with a new interior vulnerability. This vulnerability renders the man capable in faith of having Christ live His mysteries over again in the seminarian's body. From such intimacy with the Holy Trinity, a man can become "missionary."[20]

Such a life of interiority has no danger of enclosing a man in himself because every facet of spiritual direction introduces the man to a living encounter with God, who configures the seminarian into a likeness of the Beloved Son sent for the salvation of the world. God wills to likewise send such a man on mission. In being configured to the Beloved Son, the future priest resists being smothered in any egocentric, emasculating cocoon of superficial affirmation. Such malformed priests exist, of course, because they opted out of the suffering needed to become men of true interiority, ones who encountered the living God, who embraced their identity as sons beloved and sent by the Father. The *Ratio* promotes a "continuous configuration to Christ."[21] As such, a man who wants to be a priest needs to be interested in God as his primary love, and love of neighbor is a natural consequence of that primary love. Such an interest keeps a man fastened to this lifelong configuration as his deepest desire. Directors cannot short-circuit the necessity for all celibates to know their true calling in light of this configuration. As one transitional deacon noted to me, "God reached into my being; he loved me not for what I

20 *Ratio fundamentalis*, Introduction, no. 3.
21 *Ratio fundamentalis*, Introduction, no. 3.

An Ascetical Devotion • 149

do but at the level of *who I am* … that is celibacy; that is being the beloved son." This experience came to him in prayer after he had desired to understand the meaning of being a beloved son himself, and it became the experiential foundation of his life of service and sacrifice.

To adore the mysteries of Christ within the Blessed Sacrament as a regular part of daily prayer is not to get lost in the self but to deepen one's availability to the mystery of the Liturgy of the Eucharist. To get lost in this mystery further de-centers the ego, depleting and diminishing its hold upon a man as his prime fascination. As contemplation deepens, the ego's hold upon a man becomes weakened, exposed as boring and unfit as a focus for a lifetime in light of his being loved by God from the cross. Saint Bonaventure taught that living in the Word of God restores a man to his true integrity, as Christ's restorative acts toward man are pondered and internalized in faith, hope, and love.[22]

Promoting eucharistic adoration in seminary formation works to keep seminarians in reality.[23] To live in reality is to abide in the constant movement of grace that both affirms the seminarian in Divine Love and pushes him out to serve the poor. If one's being is not affirmed in love, in adoration, or if one is not growing in desire for a life of ministry, then one is not adoring the

---

22 Saint Bonaventure, *Into God: Saint Bonaventure's Itinerarium Mentis in Deum*, trans. Regis Armstrong (The Catholic University of America Press, 2020), 97.

23 *Program of Priestly Formation*, 6th ed., no. 255.

Holy Trinity. Both knowledge of being divinely loved and the call to love neighbor are the fruits of remaining with Christ. Further, adoration is a fitting act of prayer for all clergy as it consecrates them further as worshippers of God, the proper purpose of human existence. Persons both divine and human meet one another in the exchange of selves, in the mystery of self-possession unto self-communication. The seminarian who contemplates before the gift of the Body, Blood, Soul, and Divinity of Christ sits before his own image as well, his own dignity as a being who also exists within a reciprocity of love. Suffering the internalization of God's presence and offering one's own presence in return is the sacred exchange that capacitates one for priestly sacrifice. Priestly formation exists to welcome men who are willing to offer themselves as a response to the self-offering of God in Christ. To so offer themselves is to participate in that Christic sacrificial self-offering at the altar.

The priest's self-offering to God constitutes the pre-condition for "the many" (Heb 9:28) to participate in that same self-offering. At the altar, amid the gathered church, where the priest enacts the perfect offering of the high priest, Christ, the deepest reaches of human identity are opened in relation to God. Fr. Clarke observes:

> As the doctrine of the Trinity reveals, God's very nature is to be self-communicative love.... And the wonderful consequence is that we can now see that it is of the very nature of *being as*

An Ascetical Devotion • 151

such, at its highest, i.e. as personal, to be such. This is what it really means *to be* at its fullest: to be caught up in the great dynamic process of self-communication, receptivity, and return that we have called communion.[24]

The seminarian wants to be formed in the ways of knowing how to let God initiate communion and understand how his own response to this initiation constitutes his human dignity. Indeed, a response as an initiative of grace is a paradox. And the seminarian is eager to understand it: at first, he can try to control it, but soon, under the tutelage of the Holy Spirit, he realizes that he does not need to understand. Like Our Lady, he simply needs to say, "Yes." Such a "yes" is the summation of his freedom as a man. In effect, the director is leading the seminarian beyond his fears to a new level of trust in God, and preparing him to keep maturing well beyond seminary. Here, the director says, "You don't have to do anything in prayer; you simply must be vulnerable, available, readied to be affected by the presence, a presence that comes with an offer and elicits a response as your deepest identity, 'may it be done to me'." (Lk 1:38). In prayer, all humans are called to be Marian. All are simply awaiting the overshadowing that carries God's true intention toward us. God wants to live with us, He is *Emmanuel*;

---

24 W. Norris Clarke, SJ, *Person and Being* (Marquette University Press, 1993), 88–89.

152 • The Spiritual Formation of Seminarians

God wants His house full (Lk 14), full of the creatures he made in His own image. God wants to gather all men into Christ by His own power as a gift. In a particular and personal way, each seminarian who is being taught to pray is ushered into this universal desire of God toward humanity; you are desired (cf. Ps 45:12).

Adoring the mystery of Christ, that is, to "constantly drink anew from the original source, which is Jesus Christ,"[25] secures the pastoral charity at the heart of Catholic priesthood.[26] It is, indeed, eucharistic mysticism that moors priestly ministry. It is a man's dwelling prayerfully in the liturgy that is his ministry's most effective foundation. Seminary formation draws a man more deeply into a life of liturgical participation, a mystical sharing in the life, death, and resurrection of Christ. But such participation must be personal, *vulnerable*, and hence, capacitated toward ecstasy, that is, a life of going out of oneself into love of God and of others.

Such contemplative prayer is, by its nature, a call to the affectively mature. It will be very difficult for an affectively immature seminarian to rest in the receptivity that is God's love because "emotional intimacy threatens to overwhelm and disorganize [the immature] ... they are set to 'broadcast' rather than 'receive.'"[27] The affectively

---

25 Benedict XVI, *Deus caritas est*, no. 7.

26 *Program of Priestly Formation*, 6th ed., no. 12.

27 Lindsey Gibson, "How Would I Know If Someone Was

An Ascetical Devotion · 153

immature are too self-involved to contemplate and, so resist the intimate self-giving, the silence, the patient waiting for divine self-revelation and consolation. "It is inherent in the concepts of hunger and thirst that their gratification is expected from 'elsewhere', and that no one can requite himself with himself and by himself alone … man is by nature athirst … he not only needs to receive and to turn to that something perpetually, but that he also shares constantly in it"[28] The truly satisfying something is, of course, a someone, God. The affectively immature man seeks satisfaction of the self by the self and then expects all to praise him for his achieved self-involvement. To promote such a man through formation is to anticipate a parish that revolves around this man's fragile ego and undeveloped empathy. It certainly is not adoration alone that will heal immaturity, but such availability to love will bear fruit in less self-involvement and a growing fascination with God. Such fruit must be demonstrable in spiritual direction and then communicated in both counseling and human formation fora. I have noticed that it is very difficult for the self-involved to sit in adoration for very long. It appears to pain them not to be able to attend to their personal needs or perceived emergencies for that long. For the affectively immature, self-centered

---

Emotionally Immature?" *New Harbinger Publications* (July 14, 2023), https://www.newharbinger.com/blog/self-help/how-would-i-know-if-someone-was-emotionally-immature/.

28 Pieper, *Happiness and Contemplation*, 33–34.

154 · The Spiritual Formation of Seminarians

concerns prioritize their time, even if these masquerade as doing for others. Interest in another's being, even while in their presence, presents an emotional hardship for the immature. As noted earlier in this book, the seminarian who cannot suffer the death of his own concerns, ego satisfactions, will instead make his parishioners suffer by his continued self-involvement.

Thankfully, if the man is willing and his human wounds are not too deep, this tendency can be overcome through faithful reception of the Eucharist and confession, through *lectio* and the rosary, through a regular examen and through person-centered asceticism, and through the guidance of his spiritual director and the web of relationships that is seminary. Such a man will be ready for ordination, ready for ministry, ready to listen to the movements of the Spirit and be a man for others. Pastoral formation as such is not the domain of the spiritual director, but the spiritual director trains the man in prayer during seminary. Such entry into prayer is preparation for a life of pastoral ministry.

Six

Prayer and Ministry

If pastoral charity is to be internalized in seminarians, they need both to offer themselves to God for purification while also engaging the presence of the Trinity through contemplative love. There is a dual motion to such a man's interior life. He prayerfully offers himself entirely so that his self-centered habits are healed, all the while making room for God and the needs of others. "He must increase; I must decrease" (Jn 3:30). It is the director's task to recognize this dual movement as constituting a man's interior life and therefore identifying an acceptable candidate for Holy Orders. Those who resist such suffering raise a question: Do they have a true interest in being configured to Christ at the altar?

156 · The Spiritual Formation of Seminarians

Contemplation Even in Action

As we form seminarians in a love of the eucharistic liturgy, *lectio divina*, the examen, and personal eucharistic adoration (all within a context of pastoral and intellectual development), our goal is to gift the Church with men who "live in intimate and unceasing union with the Father through His Son Jesus Christ in the Holy Spirit."[1] The diocesan priest can be rightfully described as *a cleric who lives in union with the Holy Trinity unto the gift of pastoral charity*. It is this contemplative union with God birthing pastoral charity within a context of sacramental presiding that forms the nucleus of diocesan priestly spirituality. It is with this dynamic reality in mind that seminary spiritual direction seeks to achieve its ends. Every director wants to present to the Church a man who prays from the heart, is ordered by liturgy, and sent from it to embody pastoral charity. The director listens for a man's maturing appropriation of this mission as his own.

As seminaries appropriate more deeply the radical vision for seminarian spiritual formation of both the *Ratio* and the *Program of Priestly Formation*, they will come to marvel at how these texts have further concretized and developed the truth of *Optatam totius*, 8. From these ecclesial documents, we learn the key movement of the Holy Spirit within seminary formation is one of integration. In the end, the spiritual director wants the

---

1 *Optatam totius*, no. 8.

seminarian to become capable of suffering the love of God as his own moral and spiritual conversion. Such generous suffering on the part of the future priest prepares him to empathically suffer the wounds of his parishioners in a ministry of divine healing. To suffer the love of God is to be a man who wills integration, who no longer acts out of neediness or self-centeredness or from a desire to win approval but is finally self-possessed. This self-possessed man is won through the long surrender of his sins and emotional wounds into the mystery of Christ's own self-offering to the Father for the needs of humanity.

Self-possession through self-surrender is the way of spiritual and pastoral maturation. This paradoxical journey of the self toward an integrated and mature life and ministry is one of ever-deepening affective and intellectual vitality. The spiritual work of remaining in prayer long enough and deep enough to sustain a commitment to pastoral charity is a gift of *faith grounding affectivity*. "Affective love is true and mature when it has stood the test and becomes perfected in effective love."[2] Prayer

---

2 Emerich Coreth, SJ, "Contemplative in Action," *Theology Digest* 3, no. 1 (1955): 44. This is a very helpful article that aids one's thinking on how praying is related to ministerial action. However, at one point in the essay, the author promotes the idea that the more prayer permeates our whole life, the less necessary may be specific times of prayer. I would hesitate to subscribe to such a notion in light of human weakness and even more strongly in light of the witness of saints. Which saint stopped praying because he had judged himself to be permeated by it?

158 • The Spiritual Formation of Seminarians

wants to become action. The seminarian who *knows* (faith deepened by intimate prayer) he is loved by God will want to minister to others in the way he is loved by God: as a presence willing his good. No formator should be wary of a seminarian simply because he loves to pray, he wants to be with the God who called him into a celibate life. However, formators should be wary of a seminarian who expresses a love of prayer but gives no evidence of effective love toward others. Is such a man describing his experience or only telling the director what he wants to hear? There is a profound interpenetration between time with God and mature service to human need. "By their fruits you will know them" (Mt 7:20).

As the years of formation progress, spiritual directors are called into a sustained conversation with directees about the mystery of praying even while ministering, of being men of contemplation *even in action*. As one's life matures into one of divine permeation, anchored and sustained in explicit times of intimate prayer, the cleric's ministry now emerges as the fruit of communion with God and not simply as an effect of his own natural gifts and talents. The work of direction is to form a man of interiority durable enough to withstand the trials of pastoral activity. This interior man can habitually notice his own thoughts, feelings, and desires and then relate them to God in prayer. Praying in this way opens the door to experiencing the Holy Trinity in more meaningful and intimate ways. As this intimacy deepens, so does the internalization of the mystery of salvation; such internalization exists,

Prayer and Ministry • 159

then, as a reservoir from which the future cleric draws in his prayer and counsel to parishioners.

On a very practical level, spiritual direction is at the service of teaching seminarians that their relationship with God is their true foundational communion of intimacy. This truth is vital for the seminarian to ponder as he will be entering a celibate commitment that may unfortunately be devoid of clerical friendship and filled with emotional stress.[3] Without a tested and lively prayer life, we risk ordaining men who are at a loss in satisfying their need for emotional and spiritual intimacy. Further, directors should open the seminarian's imagination to the fact that Christian friendship can be found beyond the confines of their assigned rectory, especially if such becomes a house empty of the joy had in a fellowship of faith. Beyond the lack of clerical fellowship, the day-to-day sufferings of boredom or rejection or failure take a great toll on priests in their first few years after ordination. A young priest may also find that he inadequately executes administrative and human resource duties due to lack of training. New priests have also reported the burden of being overworked, feeling burnt out or disappointed with the laity or parish staff

---

3 National Association of Catholic Theological Schools and The Center for Applied Research in the Apostolate, "Enter by the Narrow Gate: Satisfaction and Challenges Among Recently Ordained Priests," (2020), https://files.ecatholic.com/2622/document.

160 • The Spiritual Formation of Seminarians

due to apathy or power struggles. He may have a poor relationship with the pastor; it is not uncommon that older priests do not know how to mentor newer priests or have no interest in doing so. In this case, the new priest can have his confidence shaken due to the absence of any "spiritual father" and the blessing one would impart. In light of all these very human problems that are certainly not rare in priestly life, settling a man into a life of intimacy with God is not some poetic ancillary avocation but an essential aspect of authentic priestly formation. Every director needs to truly encourage the seminarian to find a spiritual director after ordination and devote himself to the discipline of sharing the content of prayer and ministerial life with an experienced person of prayer bearing wisdom born from parish ministry.

To pray even while ministering is a virtue any director can begin to introduce to seminarians at an early part of their formation. It is common for men to bifurcate their spiritual lives, leaving God behind in the chapel as they go about their study and service alone. Throughout seminary spiritual direction, a man is called to become proficient at receiving the Lord's grace, even while ministering. Such receptivity of grace during self-giving deepens one's awareness that such service is never executed alone. God wants to accompany the cleric in ministry, whether that particular day ministry is experienced as "successful" or shrouded in one's own weakness and "failure." God wants to share in it all. The director needs to ask if the seminarian wants to share "all" with God. It is the

Prayer and Ministry • 161

consistent turning to the Holy Trinity in prayer, even amid ministry, that will carry a man into consolation, whether his judgment about that day's events is positive or negative. To share one's positive and negative apostolic experiences with the living God directs the seminarian to an even deeper unity between the pastoral charity of Jesus he will come to embody and the source of that charity in God.

It will be useful to the seminarian to learn during formation that he may, at times, hide aspects of his inner or apostolic life from God and, therefore, remain only partially present to Him during prayer. These areas that remain hidden may be areas of pain, failure, shame, or weakness. As long as they are hidden, they remain untouched by God's love. "Where have I not let God love me today?" is a good question to underscore, especially as it intersects with one's daily examen of consciousness. If awareness about one's day (success and failure) and possession of one's thoughts, feelings, and desires can become habituated within the seminarian, then such a habit in relation to prayer can truly assist the young priest negotiate his way around any of the negative situations mentioned above (for example, lack of clerical fellowship).

Let me explore a little further the importance of having a seminarian become more aware of his own interiority. As the seminarian matures in the ways of relating his thoughts feelings and desires to God in the concrete apostolic formational experiences of seminary, he can develop the character trait of becoming aware of his interiority.

First, in concert with any instruction on the importance of both external and interior silence, the director highlights how vital it is for the seminarian to become *conscious of himself*, to notice the stream of thoughts, feelings, and desires that course through his mind and heart daily. Such self-consciousness assists a man in giving to God his true self and standing before God vulnerable to grace. To attain such levels of intimacy with God, a man must bring both ordered and disordered desires to God. When offered to the authentic God, prayer is the safest emotional place on earth. That is, one can bring any desire to God and have His loving presence respond to it according to what is in the person's best interest. If a seminarian is not ready to share his disordered desires with God in prayer for healing, then the director waits for a day when the seminarian becomes free enough to do so. This openness can be prayed for and encouraged by the director, and likewise desired and prayed for by the seminarian, but it is not merely a matter of effort but a grace that must be received.

To stand before God in truth is the only way the interior communion with Him deepens and becomes secure on the foundation of unconditional divine love. Such growth in self-consciousness also assists a man with communal living in the seminary. Such awareness can guide the seminarian in understanding how the formation staff and peers may be receiving him as a man.

Prayer and Ministry · 163

When self-awareness grows, the need to be defensive toward any legitimate criticism decreases. In this case, when a formator might point out an area of growth for the seminarian, there is no need for defense or dejection on the seminarian's part since he already knows to some degree that aspect of himself through silent refection and the fruit of prayer. Generous time given to raising self-knowledge to a mature level serves both the interest of the Church and the man's own peaceful apprehension of his authentic self (as opposed to one based upon wishes or past prejudiced affirmations).

Second, the director moves the seminarian away from any tendency *to turn in on himself*, either in isolated introspection or for the purpose of self-consolation. Turning in on the self paves a smooth path for Satan to play with a man's mind, to offer temptations toward hate and blame of others, or hate of self. To turn in on oneself in stressful situations is normal in fallen human beings, but it must be overcome in grace. The priestly life is one of offering, offering the sacrifice of Christ and offering the self in concert with that sacrifice. Turning in on the self is the direct opposite of the priestly vocation. Any habitual self-consolation or self-concern has to be vacated, and that space has to be filled by God. "God is an approaching god, and our main job will be not so much achievement as space. 'Making space for God in order to receive'.... The emphasis is not on our forging a way, but on our getting out of the way. Progress will be measured ... by the amount

164 • The Spiritual Formation of Seminarians

of room God is given to maneuver."[4] Allowing God to nudge the ego out of the center of a man's first interest so that He might enter his heart to love and heal is priestly formation crystalized. Priestly formation as configuration to Christ is priestly formation as effecting affective maturity. To be so matured is to finally recognize that being human is to ascend to a life of being disposed to be affected by the Christ. To allow Christ to affect us in our neediness is maturity.[5]

Once a man surrenders in his neediness for Christ, he begins a journey from affective immaturity to spousal self-giving. At first, aspiring to spousal self-giving is daunting to one used to self-involvement. But allowing Christ to configure a man to His own spousal sacrifice by way of vulnerability to divine love becomes a desired path to spiritual maturity. A seminarian on this path will one day learn that his seminary formators gradually came to see a priest in the man before them. All must be shared with the Most Holy Trinity in prayer so that the man can receive all from God, that is, can receive a healed and holy humanity.

Third, a seminarian is to be instructed in how to turn toward God in dialogue with Him about the content of his consciousness. The spiritually healthy and emotionally mature man will bring his consciousness of the self in all

---

4 Iain Matthew, *The Impact of God: Soundings from St. John of the Cross* (Hodder and Stoughton, 1995), 35, 37.

5 Matthew, 137.

Prayer and Ministry • 165

its weakness (and virtue) into a conversation with God. The matter of his own interiority becomes an essential and truth-filled part of that relationship in which the seminarian dwells with God. Of course, prayer is not simply therapeutic or centered on "sharing feelings and ideas" with God, but sharing such authentic matter of real life assists in a man's growth in intimacy with God, in adhering to Him as a person. It is not opposed to listening to His voice; there is time for both sharing and receiving if one is faithful to prayer.

Communicating one's thoughts, feelings, and desires yields the fruit of intimacy. Such would be analogous to other forms of human communication (for example,the conversation and level of intimate presence found in the life of a husband and wife). God Himself revealed to humans the content of His heart through the Incarnation, and our response to such self-revelation seals the personal communion a believer has with God in an ecclesial context. Within a full relationship containing this kind of personal prayer are, of course, all the other types of prayer indicated within the tradition: "blessing, petition, intercession, thanksgiving, and praise."[6] In direction, however, the advisor is committed to teaching seminarians that prayer is primarily one's response *in love to first being loved by God*. This personal exchange—this self-revelatory prayer—is the primordial one. By way of such loving communication, we are drawn to remain in

---

6 *Catechism of the Catholic Church*, no. 2644.

166 • The Spiritual Formation of Seminarians

the Divine Presence to praise, worship, and adore He who "first loved us" (1 Jn 4:19). As noted earlier in this book, I agree with Acklin and Hicks that the contemplative aspect of prayer is "foundational and permeates the entire experience of prayer. Contemplation is not so much an elite stage of prayer ... as it is an aspect of a personal relationship.... The ... dimension of vulnerable, attentive, loving presence persists throughout the whole relationship."[7]

Seminarians cannot sustain a prayer life with God if they are not first aware that such a life informs them of their identity and even sustains their identity. Without prayer, we risk drawing our deepest identity from "this age" (Rom 12:1–2) and not from identity's sacred source. This can be true even for seminarians who outwardly express a loud "Catholic identity," but who take their identity from some partisan understanding of Catholicism or from opposition to immorality rather than as beloved sons of the Father in the Son through the Spirit. To be present to God is essential to priesthood, as this vocation calls one to preach and pray from an authentic life, one of loving and being loved by God. In the end, a seminarian's personal prayer is a mutual exchange of presences motivated and sustained by his own love for his vocation. In the early stages of formation, it is common for seminarians to discover that a large portion of their prayer consists of talking to

---

7 Acklin and Hicks, *Personal Prayer*, xxxii–xxxiii.

themselves in the presence of God. Slowly, they become conscious of this irregularity and desire to reorder their communication to engage the silent presence of the mysterious God.

Fourth, the seminarian is to remain steadfastly with God in prayer, which affords him a shift of consciousness. Commitment to prayer over time will mean a diminished interest in the self and growing fascination with God. As the relationship deepens due to such prayer, then the internalization of the beloved displaces self-involvement. In the end, all contemplatives can say "He must increase; I must decrease" (Jn 3:30). To desire to echo John the Baptist's statement is indicative of one maturing into a man of interiority. The temptation will always be to "go back to Egypt" (Nm 14:4), that is, to return to the immediate gratification of self-involvement. Mature contemplatives see plainly that such a turn is fruitless. In seminarians, such a turn indicates their knowledge and love of God is still superficial. God has yet to become their primary object of interest. Still lurking in their memory is a "payoff" on the emotional level if only they would return to those habits that produce immediate gratification. Since their contemplation is maturing in formation, they tend to lack at first reserves of virtue to resist such temptations. The seminarian's way of remaining with God and slowly denying nourishment to the ego is developmental and certainly needs the four to eight years of seminary given to him by the Church.

168 • The Spiritual Formation of Seminarians

God is known in prayer by love, and this is a love that allows itself to be purified of self-interest.[8] The ascetical life is partnered with the spiritual life as a cooperative energy aimed at asphyxiating the ego features of prayer. These features seek to hijack the practice of being in the presence of God into a familiar, routinized, and ultimately boring occasion for thinking, yet again, about the self and its needs and interests. Practices of fasting and of charity do not necessarily make prayer come more easily, but they sharpen the man's hunger for divine intimacy and thus combat self-absorption. But the director should be wary of a man who tries to give to others more than he has received; pastoral charity should not be pursued apart from prayer but built upon prayer.

Fifth, the director encourages his men to allow God's presence to be the agent for deepening their own presence toward others. Of course, this movement of mutually deepening and interpenetrating presences is the expression of the great commandment where Christ asks us to love God, neighbor, and self. As one makes room for God in prayer, His presence turns the seminarian toward the mystery of himself in both acceptance and conversion, while simultaneously noticing the needs of

---

8 See the following essay for a succinct discussion on this theme of love: Donald Haggerty, "Clarifications on the Notion of Religious Experience," in *Culture, Contemplation, and Seminary Formation*, ed. James Keating (Institute for Priestly Formation, 2018), 29–49.

others in charity. God's presence gives to the man who prays a trust that in forgetting himself, he does not lose himself. God's presence secures a man's presence to himself and to others. More and more, the man desires to be with God and in service of those in need. Prayer—when genuine—always assists a person to finally see the poor and the "poor man" within the self. It is contemplation that births ministry and sustains it. Making space for God within the human heart through prayer allows God to bring a man more deeply into God's own "space." As a result of that, the man turns toward what God desires: the company of human beings in relation to Himself.

At the end of the Parable of the Great Banquet, the master of the house reveals the intention of God toward humanity. This intention is to have fellowship (*communio*) through the Eucharist with "the ... many" (Heb 9:28). As the Master himself says, "I want my house full" (Lk 14:23). The men in formation are being configured to this intention. They are to go out and seek the lost and invite them into the mystery of God's love, the Eucharist, where healing from sin and anticipation for eternal life is known. Each seminarian is to embrace a prayer life in the desire to finally be more fascinated with God and others than with himself. The exhausting way of life which is self-involvement can finally be over, and a man can come to say as his own vocation what God says, "'What do you want me to do for you?'"(Mk 10:51). Ministry can begin only when prayer becomes a sustained reality within a man's heart because ministry is only authentic when one is sent (Mk 3:14).

To be sent, the seminarian must be immersed in relationships of truth, ones where spiritual and emotional immaturity are "wrung out" of the man in sometimes painful ways. In true encounters with persons, a man can come to know the limits of his own self-knowledge. Such failures of self-knowledge might reflect fantasy or projected perfection upon the man by others (perhaps his parents). Such distorted self-knowledge may also be reductionistic and communicate only a negative self-image to the man, an image born of emotional wounds. In both the relationship that is prayer and the relationships that are seminary, a man has the real possibility of being seen empathically. If the man is courageous in vulnerability and is received with respect and attentiveness, such a perspective will be that communion that gives him life.

Praying with Seminarians

"Spiritual Formation is directed at nourishing and sustaining communion with God and with our brothers and sisters, in the friendship of Jesus the Good Shepherd, and with an attitude of docility to the Holy Spirit."[9] If sustaining communion with God is the goal of spiritual

---

9 *Ratio fundamentalis* (2016), no. 101; *Program of Priestly Formation*, 6th ed. (2022), no. 225.

Prayer and Ministry · 171

formation in the seminary, then it is good for the spiritual director to lead a man into prayer at each scheduled direction session. Of course, most directors will open the session with a prayer, but tracking the movement of grace during the session is as important as anointing the session with prayer at the outset. Often, the Spirit will lead a man into such truth about himself and or the relationship he has with the Holy Trinity that the room fills with a profound silence, a silence with a new weight. Directors should interpret that silence as having a presence within it and invite the seminarian to remain there in this presence and receive what is being given. This silence, this fullness of presence, is being given so the seminarian can integrate whatever truth arrived in his heart into the rest of his being. The director desires to revere this precious moment. He invites the seminarian to remain in this vulnerable position of receiving the truth offered, sometimes even to the point of tears. "Let yourself be loved" is the message of this in-session shared prayer.

As the silence lightens, the director can ask the seminarian to notice and describe what just happened to him during the conversation. What did God share with him as the silence deepened? Where did God take him? What did God say about any truth received? In asking the man to give testimony, the director is giving further opportunity for grace or insight to deepen in his heart. As the director listens to the testimony, he may note that such an insight will help the formation staff to further gain knowledge of the seminarian as well. As a result, the

172 • The Spiritual Formation of Seminarians

director may ask the seminarian to consider taking the content of this full silence to another seminary forum. In doing this, the director is aware that the seminarian, as well as the Church, will benefit from any response given to the seminarian by his counselor or formation advisor.

Other spontaneous prayer moments shared between director and directee can be a regular occurrence. Another time when the director might slow the conversation down to explicitly welcome the presence of God would be when the seminarian has revealed, intentionally or inadvertently, the need for some emotional healing. Such a wound could be self-inflicted through a relentless negative litany recited by the ego. In these cases, a man has become habituated in self-condemnation, rehearsing his weaknesses and failures. Or such wounds may be emotional injuries caused by interacting with others. In either case, healing is vital since left unattended, these wounds deepen preoccupation with the self, inhibiting progress in prayer. The director offers a healing prayer or perhaps even a prayer against the machinations of Satan and then encourages the seminarian to consider sharing the contents of these wounds with both his counselor and formation staff. Follow-up with this conversation occurs in the next regularly scheduled direction meeting, where themes such as forgiveness of self and others may be explored.

Some emotional wounds are stubborn, and instead of being healed, they may have to be carried into the relationship the man has with the Holy Trinity. In this

Prayer and Ministry • 173

case, the wound does not inhibit progress in prayer but, in fact, becomes a meeting place between the seminarian and God. It becomes a place where intimacy between the two is deepened despite the wound itself remaining. Such instances might be found in the seminarian's relations with family, or in personal limits that cannot be overcome and disappoint him (such as intellectual deficiencies, physical restrictions, or lack of artistic talent), some persistent sexual temptation, personality flaws, or medical conditions that cannot be improved upon. In these areas of poverty, the director helps the seminarian see them as a rendezvous place for receiving grace.

Conclusion: Some Comments on the Director's Own Spiritual Life

St. John the apostle, the beloved disciple, leaning against the heart of Christ at the Last Supper is a classic image of the unceasing divine intimacy with which all priests should live their ministry. St. John can also be a particular icon of the spiritual director himself. Even among Jesus's top disciples and apostles, John's closeness to the Lord stands out. Fr. Christian Raab summarizes the reflections of Hans Urs von Balthasar on the icon of St. John for later priests:

> According to Balthasar, this apostle's specific mission is to mediate between the church's charismatic/subjective and official/objective poles. As

174 • The Spiritual Formation of Seminarians

> a mediator, John represents and communicates charismatic wisdom and subjective holiness to Peter, the symbol of objective office, and represents and communicates official objective authority to Mary, the symbol of the church's charismatic/subjective pole.[10]

Similarly, the role of the spiritual formator is to mediate between the hidden life of seminarians' contemplative prayer and the objective structures erected by the Church to prepare and approve of candidates for the priesthood. This does not mean that the spiritual director should try to set himself as the sole authority on the fitness of a seminarian for ordination. Like the beloved disciple on the morning of the resurrection, the spiritual director "runs ahead" to examine the man's spiritual life, but he must still wait for "Peter"—the bishop, rector, etc.— to confirm what he has seen (cf Jn 20:3–7).[11]

To be faithful to the example of St. John, the spiritual formator must be a cleric particularly close to the Lord, and willing to stay with Him through trials just as the

---

10 Raab, *Understanding the Religious Priesthood* (The Catholic University of America Press, 2021), 191. Fr. Raab follows Balthasar in proposing St. John and St. Paul as icons of religious priesthood, but St. John is also an icon for spiritual formators, for the reasons explained above.

11 This comparison is indebted to Balthasar's reading of the passage. See Raab, 194.

Prayer and Ministry · 175

beloved disciple was the only apostle to follow Jesus to the cross, so that he can help others penetrate the mystery of the Sacred Heart more profoundly. The care of the director's own spiritual life is thus paramount when considering all the elements of an effective spiritual formation program for seminarians. Obviously, those appointed to be directors have been vetted by the seminary rector and bishop and have been identified as men of competence in and commitment to the Catholic spiritual life. "Competence" is not at issue when one addresses the situation of directors slipping out of communion. Normally, such drifting is circumstantial and episodic. To prevent such drifting, the director stays in touch with his own director and commits himself to a yearly retreat and several mornings or days of reflection sought on his own volition.

Commonly, it is simply the stress of the director's own vocation that may lead him to back away from prayer or refrain from spiritual or theological reading. It may also be a type of boredom that sets in around the duty to listen to many seminarians each day rehearse the human condition before the director's mind and heart. The common struggles in prayer of seminarians can lend itself to boredom as the director listens to the same content coming from different men's hearts. The director should be on guard for the subtle presence of resentment in his heart, a sense that his "job" appears predictable or even, due to his hiddenness, unrewarding. Boredom is a sign that something has pulled the director's

176 · The Spiritual Formation of Seminarians

attention from the spiritual journey of the seminarian toward his own unmet needs; and, so, the presence of boredom invites a director to explore that condition with his or her own director. During those times when a director is sustained by a deep grace of communion with the Trinity, his listening during direction sessions is alive with interest in how God is moving in the seminarians' interior life. This lively interest can wane as the result of some unrelated pain in the director's own life; and, so, listening to the voices of seminarians simply provokes the director's own awareness of this pain and emotional isolation leading him to be bored or resentful or angry. In grace the director can ask the Lord to give him a renewed heart, a heart that listens to the hearts of seminarians as one would listen to the suffering of the poor from an empathetic heart.

Another way out of boredom or the predictability of direction is to ask for the grace of sensitivity around the movements of God both in the director's own heart and in that of the seminarian. The subtlety of God's actions can lend themselves to be overlooked leaving one to believe that God has abandoned the pray-er. Of course, faith and the experience of the director knows that this is not the case. Asking for what I call "the director's grace"—increased sensitivity to God's movements— is truly a prayer God wants to answer. In growing in such awareness, the director also grows in a desire to praise and adore and worship God even right in the midst of seminarian direction. Becoming sensitive to God in all

Prayer and Ministry • 177

His newness, even as one attends to common human concerns and challenges during direction, refreshes the soul of the director. Also, attending to what is happening in the director's own soul as he is a witness to these divine movements also enlivens the time of direction. Truly in this attention to his or her own soul the director is practicing what the director encourages the seminarian to do as well: remain in prayer even while ministering.

Attending to the movements of God anew increases the capacity for the director's own wonder at the workings of grace. One begins a day of direction in anticipation: "What will God reveal to me and my men today?" In these revelations, my own intimacy with the Holy Trinity will deepen as will my own trust and confidence that God wants to be known. The Incarnation was not an afterthought but the very movement of God's own nature—"God is love" (1 Jn 4:8). This nature is self-revelatory love: "God sent his only Son into the world so that we might have life through him" (1 Jn 4:9). The director—perhaps more than many in the Church—has a front row seat in watching God be God in the personal lives of believers: "This is how we know that we remain in him and he in us, that he has given us of his Spirit" (1 Jn 4:13). In his prayerful attention to the lives of seminarians, the director is privileged to literally see persons being loved by God: "We have come to know and to believe in the love God has for us" (1 Jn 4:16). Even such a ministry may, of course, be subject to human weakness and limitation but through meditation and prayer and good counsel it

178 · The Spiritual Formation of Seminarians

may not take long to have a new zeal revived: "There is no fear in love, but perfect love drives out fear" (1 Jn 4:18).

Another struggle within direction may come from a clash of personalities between director and seminarian. There is always the option to request that the seminarian find a new director as such a clash, if chronic, may impede the seminarian's hope that direction will yield a deeper intimacy with God. The ironic part of some of these personality clashes, however, is that in the clash itself sometimes God has a plan. To release a seminarian too soon to another director may in fact be just the thing that impedes his hoped-for divine intimacy. It is the direction relationship itself that carries the spiritual and affective development of the seminarian. On occasion, to welcome the man into direction who is not at first attractive in character and disposition is simply to recognize the labor the director is contracted to enter. It will be work to remain with this man in conversation, but fidelity to that conversation will transform those unattractive traits. The director sees the immaturity but also the possibility for transformation; now he is invited in grace to choose the welfare of the seminarian and keep directing him toward God and conversion of life. In the meantime, the director is working out his own growth and salvation in exhibiting such love and perseverance for the good of the Church. As the director matures in his own vocation, this type of situation regarding personality clash becomes part of the awe he feels over the transfiguring power of prayer. The once uninviting young man has become a priest, and a large part of that movement from uninviting seminarian to competent priest happened in the love and suffering of spiritual direction.

Finally, as directors serving diocesan seminarians and sometimes priests, we run into what I call the diocesan blind spot. This blind spot prevents some clerics from seeing the need to commit to ever deepening prayer throughout a ministerial life. Some priests may even say that their ministry is by nature too active for contemplative prayer. It is a ministry that draws its strength from sacramental service and not contemplative prayer. We need the grace of the sacraments, of course. For directors, however, this blind spot may subtly influence us to lower our expectations around diocesan clergy entering a life of contemplative prayer. While there really are challenges within parish ministry that discourage committing to a life of deeper relational prayer, directors excel when they point out the true benefits of such prayer for clergy who persevere. Not the least of these benefits is a life of congruent integrity, of being a preacher of the word of God as well as a man who communes with that same living word relationally as his first love interest. The fruit of such an interior life is an ongoing gift to Christ's first interest, the parish flock such a priest presides over and shepherds.

The ministry of seminary spiritual director is a privileged mission sustained by grace and the ever-growing insight into the human drama of salvation attained by the

180 · The Spiritual Formation of Seminarians

director as he serves the earnest seminarian seated before him in conversation. From this position the director's role is simple in its essence: he is to be one who notices obstacles between the seminarian and his deepest desire to be one with the Most Holy Trinity. In this noticing the director assists the seminarian in attaining his own freedom before God. "Jesus is always listening—listening to see if he hears our deepest voice rising above the tumult of the world and of our passions."[12] The director helps the seminarian find that voice. In this way, he helps to gift the Church with men after the Lord's own heart, men who are healed mystic teachers, and witnesses to the Word made flesh.

> What was from the beginning,
>   what we have heard,
>   what we have seen with our eyes,
>   what we looked upon
>   and touched with our hands
>   concerns the Word of life—
> for the life was made visible;
>   we have seen it and testify to it
>   and proclaim to you the eternal life
>   that was with the Father and was made visible
>   to us—

---

12 Erasmo Leiva-Merikakis, *The Way of the Disciple* (Ignatius Press, 2003), 78.

what we have seen and heard
  we proclaim now to you,
  so that you too may have fellowship with us;
  for our fellowship is with the Father
  and with his Son, Jesus Christ.
We are writing this so that our joy may be complete.
(1 Jn 1:1–4)

BIBLIOGRAPHY

Acklin, Thomas, OSB, and Boniface Hicks, OSB. *Personal Prayer: A Guide for Receiving the Father's Love.* Emmaus Road Publishing, 2019.

Aschenbrenner, George, SJ. *Quickening the Fire in Our Midst: The Challenge of Diocesan Priestly Spirituality.* Loyola Press, 2002.

Augustine, St. *Confessions.* Translated by John K. Ryan. Image, 1960.

Aumann, Jordan. *Spiritual Theology.* Bloomsbury, 1980.

Balthasar, Hans Urs von. *Engagement with God.* Ignatius Press, 2008.

Balthasar, Hans Urs von. *Prayer.* Ignatius Press, 1986.

Benedict XVI, Pope. "Address to Clergy." Freising Cathedral. September 15, 2006.[1]

Benedict XVI, Pope. "Address to the Participants in the International Congress Organized to Commemorate the 40th Anniversary of the Dogmatic Constitution on Divine Revelation *Dei Verbum.*" September 16, 2005.

---

1 All Vatican documents available at vatican.va unless otherwise noted.

184 · Bibliography

Benedict XVI, Pope Emeritus. *Called to Holiness: On Love, Vocation, and Formation*, edited by Pietro Rossotti. The Catholic University of America Press, 2017.

Benedict XVI, Pope. "Chrism Mass." April 13, 2006.

Benedict XVI, Pope. *Deus caritas est*. Encyclical Letter. December 25, 2005.

Benedict XVI, Pope. "General Audience." May 16, 2012.

Benedict XVI, Pope. *Jesus of Nazareth: From the Baptism in the Jordan to the Transfiguration*. Doubleday, 2007.

Benedict XVI, Pope. *Light of the World: The Pope, the Church, and the Signs of the Times*. Ignatius Press, 2010.

Benedict XVI, Pope. "Meeting with Clergy." May 25, 2006.

Benedict XVI, Pope. *Sacramentum caritatis*. Post-Synodal Apostolic Exhortation. February 22, 2007.

Benner, David G. *Surrender to Love: Discovering the Heart of Christian Spirituality*. InterVarsity Press, 2015.

Bonaventure, Saint. *Into God: Saint Bonaventure's Itinerarium Mentis in Deum*. Translated by Regis Armstrong. The Catholic University of America Press, 2020.

Bouyer, Louis. *The Christian Mystery: From Pagan Myth to Christian Mysticism*. Saint Bede Abbey Press, 1990.

Boylan, Eugene. *Difficulties in Mental Prayer*. Christian Classics, 2010.

Cabasilas, Nicholas. *The Life in Christ*, Ex-Monastery Library edition. St. Vladimir's Seminary Press, 1997.

Cantalamessa, Raniero. *The Mystery of Easter*. Liturgical Press, 1993.

Cardó, Daniel. *What Does It Mean to Believe? Faith in the Thought of Joseph Ratzinger.* Emmaus Academic, 2020.

Catechism of the Catholic Church. USCCB Publishing, 2000.

Cavadini, John. "Celibacy in the Church and the Priesthood." *Church Life Journal* (June 2, 2023). https://churchlifejournal.nd.edu/articles/celibacy-in-the-church-and-the-priesthood.

Clarke, W. Norris, SJ. *Person and Being.* Marquette University Press, 1993.

Congregation for the Clergy. *Ratio fundamentalis institutionis sacerdotalis*: The Gift of the Priestly Vocation. December 8, 2016.

Ciraulo, Jonathan. *The Eucharistic Form of God: Hans Urs von Balthasar's Sacramental Theology.* University of Notre Dame Press, 2022.

Cooper, Adam. *Holy Eros: A Liturgical Theology of the Body.* Angelico Press, 2014.

Coreth, Emerich, SJ. "Contemplative in Action." *Theology Digest* 3, no. 1 (1955): 37–45.

Cozzens, Andrew H. *A Living Image of the Bridegroom: The Priesthood and the Evangelical Counsels.* Institute for Priestly Formation, 2020.

Daniélou, Jean. *Prayer: The Mission of the Church.* Eerdmans, 1996.

Dicastery for Communication. *Towards a Full Presence: A Pastoral Reflection on Engagement with Social Media.* May 28, 2023.

Evagrius. *Praktikos and Chapters on Prayer.* Cistercian Publications, 1981.

186 · Bibliography

Fagerberg, David. *The Liturgical Cosmos: The World Through the Lens of the Liturgy*. Emmaus Academic, 2023.

Fagerberg, David. *Liturgical Mysticism*. Emmaus Academic, 2019.

Fagerberg, David W. *On Liturgical Asceticism*. The Catholic University of America Press, 2013.

Feingold, Lawrence. *The Eucharist: Mystery of Presence, Sacrifice, and Communion*. Emmaus Academic, 2018.

Feingold, Lawrence. "The Role of Beauty in Seminary Formation." In *As a Priest Thinks, So He Is: The Role of Philosophy in Seminary Formation*, edited by Beth Rath McGough and Patricia Pintado-Murphy. IPF Publications 2023.

Fitzgerald, Allan D., ed. *Augustine Through the Ages: An Encyclopedia*. Eerdmans, 1999.

Florea, Eugene. *The Priest's Communion with Christ: Dispelling Functionalism*. Institute for Priestly Formation, 2018.

Francis, Pope. "Message of the Holy Father Pope Francis Signed by Cardinal Secretary of State for the Meeting with Seminarians from France." January 12, 2023.

Francis, Pope. "Address of His Holiness to the Community of the Archepiscopal Seminary of Naples." Feb. 16, 2024.

Franks, Angela. "Identity and the Trinitarian Imago." Academy of Catholic Theology Annual Meeting. May 23–25, 2023.

Gallagher, Timothy. *Praying the Liturgy of the Hours: A Personal Journey*. Crossroad, 2014.

Gallagher, Timothy, OMV. *The Discernment of Spirits: An Ignatian Guide for Everyday Living*. The Crossroad Publishing Company, 2005.

Gibson, Lindsey. "How Would I Know If Someone Was Emotionally Immature?" *New Harbinger Publications*. July 14, 2023. https://www.newharbinger.com/blog/self-help/how-would-i-know-if-someone-was-emotionally-immature/.

Goulding, Gill, CJ. "Holiness of Mind and Heart: The Dynamic Imperative of Conversion and Contemplation for the Study of Theology." In *Entering into the Mind of Christ: The True Nature of Theology*, edited by James Keating. Institute for Priestly Formation, 2014.

Granados, José. *Introduction to Sacramental Theology: Signs of Christ in the Flesh*. The Catholic University of America Press, 2021.

Griffiths, Paul. "Ora et Labora: Christians Don't Need Leisure." *Church Life Journal* (July 18, 2018).

Haggerty, Donald. "Clarifications on the Notion of Religious Experience." In *Culture, Contemplation, and Seminary Formation*, edited by James Keating. Institute for Priestly Formation, 2018.

Haggerty, Donald. *Contemplative Enigmas: Insights and Aid on the Path to Deeper Prayer*. Ignatius Press, 2020.

Hildebrand, Dietrich von. *The Heart: An Analysis of Human and Divine Affectivity*. St. Augustine Press, 2007.

188 · Bibliography

Imbelli, Robert P. *Rekindling the Christic Imagination: Theological Meditations for the New Evangelization.* Liturgical Press, 2014.

Janczuk, Weronika. "The Place of the Heart in Integral Human Formation." *Logos* 21, no. 1 (2018): 118–47.

John Paul II, Pope. *Novo millenio ineunte.* Apostolic Letter. January 6, 2001.

John Paul II, Pope. *Pastores dabo vobis.* Post-Synodal Apostolic Exhortation. March 25, 1992.

John Paul II, Pope. *Redemptoris custos.* Apostolic Exhortation. August 15, 1989.

John Paul II, Pope. *Redemptoris mater.* Encyclical Letter. March 25, 1987.

Keating, James. *Configured to Christ: On Spiritual Direction and Clergy Formation.* Emmaus Road Publishing, 2021.

Keating, James, ed. *Entering into the Mind of Christ: The True Nature of Theology.* Institute for Priestly Formation, 2014.

Keating, James. "From Fantasy to Contemplation: Seminarians and Formation in a Paschal Imagination." *Nova et Vetera*, English edition 16, no. 2 (2018): 367–76.

Keating, James, ed. *Lectio Divina: Assimilating the Holy Word in Seminary Formation.* Institute for Priestly Formation, 2023.

Keating, James, ed. *A Positive and Stable Masculine Identity: Directions in the Formation of Seminarians.* IPF Publications, 2021.

Keating, James. *Resting on the Heart of Christ: The Vocation and Spirituality of the Seminary Theologian.* Institute for Priestly Formation, 2009.

Keating, James. "Sexual Integrity in the Formation of Seminarians." In *Sex and the Spiritual Life: Reclaiming Integrity, Wholeness, and Intimacy,* edited by Patricia Cooney Hathaway. Ave Maria Press, 2020.

Keating, James. "Silence as Participation in Worship." *The Priest* (June 15, 2022). https://thepriest.com/2022/06/15/silence-as-participation-in-worship/.

Kheriaty, Aaron, and John Cihak. *The Catholic Guide to Depression: How the Saints, the Sacraments, and Psychiatry Can Help You Break Its Grip and Find Happiness Again.* Sophia Institute Press, 2012.

Kriegshauser, Laurence, OSB. "Western Monastic Tradition of *Lectio Divina* and Seminary Formation." In *Piercing the Clouds: Lectio Divina and Preparation for Ministry,* edited by Kevin Zilverburg and Scott Carl. Saint Paul Seminary Press, 2021.

Laird, Martin, OSA. *A Sunlit Absence: Silence, Awareness, and Contemplation.* Oxford University Press, 2011.

Leiva-Merikakis, Erasmo. *The Way of the Disciple.* Ignatius Press, 2003.

Lynch, Christina. *Born Digital: Psychological Perspectives of Human and Spiritual Formation in the Digital Age.* Published by the author, 2022.

Magrassi, Mariano, OSB. *Praying the Bible: An Introduction to Lectio Divina.* Liturgical Press, 1998.

Bibliography

Matthew, Iain. *The Impact of God: Soundings from St. John of the Cross*. Hodder and Stoughton, 1995.

McCormack, Edward J. *A Guide to Formation Advising for Seminary Faculty: Accompaniment, Participation, and Evaluation*. The Catholic University of America Press, 2020.

McGinn, Bernard. *The Foundations of Mysticism: Origins to the Fifth Century*. Crossroad, 1992.

McInroy, Mark J. "Karl Rahner and Hans Urs von Balthasar." In *The Spiritual Senses: Perceiving God in Western Christianity*, edited by Paul Gavrilyuk and Sarah Coakley. Cambridge University Press, 2013.

National Association of Catholic Theological Schools and The Center for Applied Research in the Apostolate. "Enter by the Narrow Gate: Satisfaction and Challenges Among Recently Ordained Priests." 2020), https://files.ecatholic.com/2622/document.

National Conference of Catholic Bishops (NCCB), *The Program of Priestly Formation*. NCCB, 1971.

Nepil, John. "A Miracle of Grace: Hans Urs von Balthasar's Vision of Priestly Spirituality." *Communio: International Catholic Review* 49, no. 1 (2022): 58–79.

Office for the Liturgical Celebrations of the Supreme Pontiff. "To Enter into the Christian Mystery Through the Rites and Prayers." September 7, 2010.

O'Keefe, Mark, OSB. *Learned, Experienced, and Discerning: St. Teresa of Avila and St. John of the Cross on Spiritual Direction.* Liturgical Press, 2020.

Patrón Wong, Jorge Carlos. *Foundations of Priestly Formation.* http://www.clerus.va/content/dam/clerus/Dox/Conference%20-%20Foundations%20of%20Priestly%20Formation.pdf (accessed 9/16/2022).

Pieper, Josef. *Happiness and Contemplation.* St. Augustine Press, 1998.

Pieper, Josef. *Leisure: The Basis of Culture.* Ignatius Press, 2009.

Raab, Christian. *Understanding the Religious Priesthood.* The Catholic University of America Press, 2021.

Ragazzi, Grazia Mangano. *Obeying the Truth: Discretion in the Spiritual Writings of Saint Catherine of Siena.* Oxford University Press, 2014.

Ratzinger, Joseph Cardinal. *Behold the Pierced One.* Ignatius Press, 1986.

Ratzinger, Joseph. *Pilgrim Fellowship of Faith: The Church as Communion.* Ignatius Press, 2005.

Ratzinger, Joseph Cardinal. "Some Perspectives on Priestly Formation Today." In *The Catholic Priest as Moral Teacher and Guide: Proceedings of Symposium Held at St. Charles Borromeo Seminary, Overbrook, Pennsylvania, January 17–20, 1990.* Ignatius Press, 1990.

Sacred Congregation for Catholic Education. "Circular Letter Concerning Some of the More Urgent

192 · Bibliography

Aspects of Spiritual Formation in Seminaries" [Jan. 6, 1980]. *Origins* 9, no. 38 (March 6, 1980): 610–19. Available at https://www.usccb.org/beliefs-and-teachings/vocations/priesthood/priestly-formation/church-documents-for-priestly-formation.

Seith, Christopher J. *Rekindling Wonder: Touching Heaven in a Screen Saturated World*. En Route Books and Media, 2022.

Sorg, Dom Rembert, OSB. *Holy Work: A Theology of Manual Labor*. Pio Decima Press, 1952.

Spadaro, Antonio, SJ. "A Big Heart Open to God: An Interview with Pope Francis." *America Magazine* (September 30, 2013). https://www.americamagazine.org/faith/2013/09/30/big-heart-open-god-interview-pope-francis.

Studzinski, Raymond, OSB. *Reading to Live: The Evolving Practice of Lectio Divina*. Liturgical Press, 2009.

Štrukelj, Anton. *Kneeling Theology*. The Catholic University of America Press, 2023.

Toups, David. *Reclaiming Our Priestly Character*. Institute for Priestly Formation, 2008.

United States Conference of Catholic Bishops. *Program of Priestly Formation*, 6th ed. USCCB, 2022.

Vatican Council II. *Optatam totius*. Decree on Priestly Training. October 28, 1965.

Wilken, Robert Louis. "Blessed Passion of Love: The Affections, the Church Fathers, and the Christian

Life." In *The Spirit, the Affections, and the Christian Tradition*, edited by Dale M. Coulter and Amos Yong. University of Notre Dame Press, 2016.

Williamson, Peter S. "Preparing Seminarians for the Ministry of the Word in Light of *Verbum Domini*." In *Verbum Domini and the Complementarity of Exegesis and Theology*, edited by Father Scott Carl. Eerdmans, 2015.

Scriptural Index

Numbers, Book of
    14:4 — 167
Kings, First Book of
    19:12 — 106
Psalms
    27:7–9, 14 — 29
    37:7 — 111
    45:12 — 152
    62:9 — 7
Matthew, Gospel of
    1:23 — 57
    1:24–25 — 84n22
    4:19 — 78
    7:20 — 158
    7:26–27 — 50
    11:28 — 74, 108
Mark, Gospel of
    3:13–14 — 58, 143, 170
    10:51 — 169
Luke, Gospel of
    1:38 — 151
    2:19 — 28
    2:35 — 28
    10:38–42 — 55–56
    13:3 — 7
    14 — 152
    14:23 — 87, 169
    14:27, 28, 33 — 50–51
    15:11–32 — 18n26
    15:19–20 — 87

John, Gospel of
    1:1, 14 — 126n1
    3:30 — 155, 167
    4:32–34 — 117
    6:63 — 84n22
    10:10 — 45–46, 92, 132
    14:6 — x, 45, 125
    15:5 — 6, 55
    18:37, 38 — 125n1
    20:3–7 — 174
Acts of the Apostles
    1:2 — 45
    1:25 — 52, 136
Romans, Paul's Letter to
    6:6 — 51
    12:1–2 — 74, 121, 133, 166
Corinthians, Paul's First
  Letter to
    3:11 — 50
Corinthians, Paul's Second
  Letter to
    10:5 — 146
Galatians, Paul's Letter to
    5:1 — 19
Colossians, Paul's Letter to
    3:1, 3–4 — 18–19, 72
Thessalonians, Paul's First
  Letter to
    5:17 — 56

196 · Index

Timothy, Paul's Second
  Letter to
    2:13 88n24
Hebrews, Letter to the
    9:28 150, 169
    10:22 22
    12:11 137
John, First Letter of
    1:1–4 181
    4:8–9, 13, 16 177
    4:18 119, 178
    4:19 166

Index

Aschenbrenner, George, SJ, 140

Augustine, Saint, 73–74, 116, 135

   Confessions, 13n17, 26n34, 73n16

affectivity, 5, 11–13, 23, 68–74, 90–92, 107–8, 129, 152–53, 157, 164

asceticism, 111, 143–45

Balthasar, Hans Urs von, 5, 15, 40n17, 46n28, 69n10, 71, 146n19, 173, 174n10

Benedict XVI, Pope, 7, 38n14, 62n2, 63n4, 94–95, 97n1, 97n2, 107, 110n12, 113, 123, 134, 152n25

   See also Ratzinger, Joseph

Bonaventure, Saint, 149

Catechism of the Catholic Church

   no. 358: 16n22

   no. 390: 16n23

   no. 1324: 111n14

   no. 1392: 100n5

   no. 1394: 100n5

   no. 1436: 100n5

   no. 2015: 144n14

   no. 2644: 165n6

celibacy, 21–22, 58–59, 70, 77–84, 112

Clarke, Norris, SJ, 150–51

contemplation, 14, 24–26, 34–35, 45–46, 54, 77, 81, 84–85, 92–95

Eucharist, 27, 40–41, 97–113, 152, 169

Evagrius, 61

examen, 27, 139–43, 147, 154, 161

Fagerberg, David, 10, 20n28, 30n1, 45n26, 67n6, 111, 144n15

Francis, Pope, ix, 9, 36–37, 94, 126n1

Franks, Angela, 18n26, 134–35

Goulding, Gill, CJ, 13

Griffiths, Paul, 16–17

Haggerty, Donald, 69n8, 168n8

Hildebrand, Dietrich von, 22–24

human formation, 16, 30, 47

198 · Index

intellectual knowledge, 33,
44, 65–66, 121–22
Institute for Priestly
Formation, xi, 11n16,
14n18, 26n34, 36n10,
41n18, 67n6, 69n9,
122n23, 168n8

John Paul II, Pope, 2–3,
5, 11–12, 14–15, 32n4,
83n20, 84n22, 113–14
See also Pastores dabo vobis
Joseph, Saint, 84n22

Lectio Divina, 120–24, 126–28,
132–38

Martha and Mary, 56–57, 65
Mary, Blessed Virgin
Immaculate, 28
Magnficat, 134
as model of "yes" to God,
151
School of, 138
symbol of church's
charismatic/subjective
pole, 174
maturity, 2, 5, 11–12, 48–49,
62–63, 81, 92, 164

obedience, 5, 13, 70, 80, 117
Optatam totius, 53n37, 156

Pastores dabo vobis, 2–5,
11–12, 15, 35n9, 48n32,

52n35, 53n37, 70n11,
79n18, 102n7
Pieper, Josef, 17n24, 27n37,
153n28
prayer, 26, 30–36, 39, 46,
53–57, 67–71, 82–87,
89–92, 112–18, 126–34,
157–62, 165–70
Program of Priestly Formation,
11n15, 20n27, 27n35,
27n36, 38, 42n19–20,
44n23–24, 47n29–31,
53n37, 137n10, 138n11,
149n23, 152n26, 156, 170n9

Raab, Christian, 173–74
Ratio fundamentalis, 37–39,
43n21, 47n29, 47n31,
48–50, 52, 53n36, 62n3,
79n18, 97n3, 121–22,
145n17, 148, 156, 170n9
Ratzinger, Joseph, 34n6,
40n16, 98n4
rosary, 137–39

spiritual direction, xi, 34, 45,
47, 73, 79–80, 105, 118,
148, 156, 159–60

technology, digital, 17, 44,
75, 107, 116

Vatican Council II. *See*
Optatam totius

From Saint Paul Seminary Press at cuapress.org

Piercing the Clouds
Lectio Divina and Preparation for Ministry
Edited by Kevin Zilverberg and Scott Carl

The Revelation of Your Words
The New Evangelization and the Role of the Seminary Professor
of Sacred Scripture
Edited by Kevin Zilverberg and Scott Carl

Verbum Domini and the Complementarity of
Exegesis and Theology
Edited by Scott Carl

The Word of Truth, Sealed by the Spirit
Perspectives on the Inspiration and Truth of Sacred Scripture
Edited by Matthew C. Genung and Kevin Zilverberg

Also from The Catholic University of America Press

A Guide to Formation Advising for Seminarians
&
A Guide to Formation Advising for Seminary Faculty
Accompaniment, Participation, and Evaluation

by Deacon Edward J. McCormack
Foreword by Ronald D. Witherup, PSS

Contemplation and the Cross
A Catholic Introduction to the Spiritual Life

by Thomas Joseph White, OP

Mysteries of the Lord's Prayer: Wisdom from the Early Church

by John Gavin, SJ
Foreword by George Weigel

Growing into God: The Fathers of the Church
on Christian Maturity

by John Gavin, SJ
Foreword by Angela Franks

Kneeling Theology

by Anton Štrukelj
Foreword by Cardinal Christoph Schonborn

Meditation as Spiritual Therapy
Bernard of Clairvaux's De consideratione
by Matthew R. McWhorter

The True Christian Life
Thomistic Reflections on Divinization, Prudence,
Religion, and Prayer
by Ambroise Gardeil, OP
Translated by Matthew K. Minerd
Foreword by Matthew Levering

The Priesthood, Mystery of Faith
Priestly Ministry in the Magisterium of John Paul II
by Nilson Leal de Sá, CB
Foreword by Cardinal José Saraiva Martins

Priestly Celibacy: Theological Foundations
by Gary B. Selin

Understanding the Religious Priesthood
History, Controversy, Theology
by Christian Raab, OSB
Foreword by Brian E. Daley, SJ

A Spiritual Theology of the Priesthood
The Mystery of Christ and the Mission of the Priest
by Dermot Power